RETIRE a WINNER!

*Live the Lifestyle and Leave
the Legacy YOU Want*

RETIRE a WINNER!

*Live the Lifestyle and Leave
the Legacy YOU Want*

**Dean Barber,
Michael E. Brown,
John Daley**

Retire a Winner!
Live the Lifestyle and Leave the Legacy YOU Want

Copyright © MMXI by Dean Barber, Michael E. Brown, John Daley

Published by:
BBD Publishing
Clifton Park, NY 12065

Page layout by Ad Graphics, Inc., Tulsa, OK 74145

Printed in the United States of America

Library of Congress Control Number: 2011900932

ISBN (hard cover): 978-0-9832905-0-6
ISBN (soft cover): 978-0-9832905-1-3

TABLE OF CONTENTS

DISCLAIMER

Financial planning is challenging to begin with. Planning distributions from IRAs and Qualified Plans is even more difficult due to the inevitable changes in our personal circumstances and the ever-evolving regulations we face. This book is meant to explain common scenarios and planning principles given the current best practices. Hypothetical examples are used throughout the book for illustrative purposes only. Returns shown are not indicative of any particular investment. Unless otherwise indicated, the examples assume reinvestment of dividends with no consequence of fees or taxes. Keep in mind that investments will fluctuate with changes in market conditions. This book in no way discusses all of the alternatives available to investors. It reflects our opinions, and is subject to our own limitations. These opinions are not intended to provide specific advice and should not be construed as recommendations for any individual. This book is published with the understanding that the authors are not engaged in rendering legal or tax services. While designed to provide accurate information on retirement plan distributions, the services of competent law and tax professionals should be sought prior to executing any strategy. Investments involve risk including the potential for loss of the principal amount invested. Please remember that investment decisions should be based on an individual's goals, time horizon, and tolerance for risk.

Acknowledgments

There are many people who deserve our thanks for helping us to complete this book:

First and foremost, we would like to extend our thanks to a pioneer in the retirement distribution world—Ed Slott, CPA, author of *The Retirement Savings Time Bomb...and How to Defuse It* and *Parlay Your IRA into a Family Fortune.* Our professional relationship with Ed Slott has given us the confidence to even attempt to write this book, and we can't thank him enough.

A big thanks as well to Dave Buckwald, one of the most knowledgeable people we know on the subject of insurance, for sharing his insights with us on the use of life insurance as a valuable wealth-protection tool.

Our deep thanks also go to nationally known speaker and elder law expert Harley Gordon for guiding us through the often-emotional subject of long-term care and disability insurance in financial planning for families.

We'd like to give a special thanks to Caryn Kennedy, an expert on financial planning for those affected by divorce—specifically women.

Another big thanks goes to Madison Wealth executive assistant Mary Ellsworth for her organizational skills and her determination to keep us on schedule and meeting our deadlines for this book.

We also would like to thank Jim and Barbara Weems, who consult with business owners like us who want to write a book of their own. They helped us in everything from book design and typesetting to printing and publication of a book we can be proud of. You can find them at www.theBookproducer.com, or call them at 1-800-368-6196.

And last but not least, we want to thank John McCarty for honchoing this project through to a successful conclusion.

INTRODUCTION

An Easily Digestible Guide

As financial advisors who work day in and day out with people who are about to retire, or who have already retired, we keep running across the same questions about IRAs and 401(k)s. We also consistently encounter the same misunderstandings about them—from both our clients and, even sometimes, their other advisors.

So we looked for a quick reference book that would answer people's questions without boring them to death. Many of the books we found were entertaining but lacked substance, or were overly dense and impossible to read. Only the most motivated reader can plow through a book filled with IRS regulations, calculations and discussions of mortality tables and still be motivated to plan for the future.

So, we wrote this book with one goal: to provide an easily digestible guide to deciding, for example, whether to keep your 401(k) with your former employer or how to pass retirement assets to the next generation while minimizing estate taxes on those assets.

Typically when faced with financial decisions, most of us tend to take the path of least resistance. This typically means that we make those decisions by *not* making them. That's the problem—because by accepting the default position, especially with regard to retirement, you never know if you could have achieved greater financial security. You'll always wonder. Well, after reading this book, you will have a better understanding of the options available to you.

Many people rely on family, friends, or their previous employer's human resources department for advice on their retirement plan. That's where the problem begins. You wouldn't rely on the same person to do your taxes and fill a cavity, would you? No, you'd go to a dentist for your filling, and to a tax preparer for your filing.

The same is true with your retirement savings. Understanding the many complicated aspects of an IRA rollover and the different IRA management strategies requires a specialist, too. Even if you retire from the best company in the world, and have invested wisely at each stage of the game, you may still need guidance.

Still, technical knowledge alone isn't always enough. You should choose an advisor who is not only technically competent, but who also has your best interests in mind. Most of the retirees we've worked with have lives that echo a similar pattern. They have worked hard for many years. Their work was rewarded, often with useful stock that became very valuable over the years. These men and women don't have the multi-million dollar portfolios that private bankers or high-flying investment managers pursue, but they do have healthy and substantial savings. They need (and deserve) the same good advice as their wealthier neighbors. We live in a country of great abundance. But we also live in a country filled with considerable threats to a comfortable retirement. Armed with the right knowledge about 401(k)s and IRAs, every retiree can have a winning strategy. This book will show you the way.

How to Use this Book

The following descriptions of each chapter will lead you to those chapters that are of particular relevance to your specific situation at this point in time.

For example, if you're not sure whether to "stretch" your IRA, or even what that concept is and how it works, but don't think you will need to use all the money in your retirement plan or IRA, Chapter 4 is for you. Others of you may skip elsewhere to those chapters that are more applicable to you. So, knowing how busy you are, please be sure to read these descriptions to see which chapters are the must-reads for you.

- Chapter 1 ("You Too Can Have a Richly Rewarding Retirement") is a MUST-READ because it explains the urgency to plan, lists all the asset classes available to build a solid plan, explores the tools and teamwork needed to help produce significant results, and the potentially dire consequences of not having a plan.

- Chapter 2 ("The Starting Gate") details the decisions you will face as you prepare to retire or to leave one employer for another. Whether you're just thinking about it or are already out the door, this chapter will help you clarify your financial goals.

- Chapter 3 ("Three Winners in the Distribution Race") is for you if you have special planning needs (for example, most of your money is in your employer's company stock), were born before 1936, and are retiring young.

- Chapter 4 ("Down the 'Stretch'") is for those of you who probably will never spend all the money in your IRA (most people don't). For you, it is vital to understand the "stretch" IRA: what it is, what it does, when it works well, and how to avoid any threats to its success.

- Chapter 5 ("Cashing Out: Minimum Distribution Rules") examines how to manage the distribution planning of your IRA, whether for your own future spending or for your beneficiaries, in order to minimize taxes and maximize your legacy.

- Chapter 6 ("A Superfecta: The Roth IRA") explores the tax-free pluses of this increasingly popular retirement vehicle, from contributing and converting, to recharacterizing and everything in between that you need to know about the Roth.

- Chapter 7 ("The Finish Line: Estate Planning for Large IRAs") shows how to keep as much of your retirement wealth as possible in the family by maximizing income tax deductions and minimizing estate taxes on that wealth after you're gone.

- Chapter 8 ("Your Retirement Plan Checklist") shows how to make sure you and your advisors have covered all the key points of income, tax, asset, and risk planning so that nothing falls through the cracks in creating your plan.

Defend Your Assets

Whether you are a grandparent or a parent intent on protecting family assets for future generations or a spouse protecting your soul mate, you will have made great progress defending your assets from unnecessary taxes by absorbing the information in this book.

Perhaps the most significant conclusion we have reached throughout the writing process is the importance of *details*. We can't stress enough how critical it is for you and your family to concentrate on the *details of retirement planning* that all too many of us tend to ignore (such as making a will) or just take for granted (e.g., believing that a will is all you need). Use the tools in this book to examine your personal situation and the minute particulars that will ultimately decide the fate of your retirement nest egg. Don't forget that the *most important* aspect of retirement planning is to ensure that the distribution of your assets is made according to *your* wishes—to the right people at the right time and in the right way. So, make sure you give as much thought to it as you do to saving on your taxes. Don't become another of those horror stories about hard working couples who could not fulfill their retirement dreams because of poor planning and a depreciated fortune. Proper planning makes the unpredictable more predictable and eliminates money from falling through the cracks.

It is our hope that this book will help you become aware of and open to the possibilities available to you and your family, enabling you to make your most important dreams come true with proper retirement planning.

Dean Barber, RFC
Barber Financial Group
13550 West 95th Street, Lenexa, KS 66215
Office: 913.393.1000 • Toll Free: 888.848.8003
retire@barberfinancialgroup.com
www.barberfinancialgroup.com

Michael E. Brown, AIFA, CFP, CIMA
Madison Wealth Managers
646 Plank Road, Suite 200, Clifton Park, NY 12065
Office: 518.348.7770 • Toll Free: 888.376.6460
info@madisonmanagers.com
www.madisonmanagers.com

John Daley, AIF
Madison Wealth Managers
646 Plank Road, Suite 200, Clifton Park, NY 12065
Office: 518.348.7770 • Toll Free: 888.376.6460
info@madisonmanagers.com
www.madisonmanagers.com

CHAPTER 1

YOU TOO CAN HAVE A RICHLY REWARDING RETIREMENT

~

HORSE SENSE
. . . .

*Don't assume that retirement planning is only for the super rich. It's for everyone who has loved ones and can't afford to make expensive mistakes. Only the very affluent can afford to absorb large stock market losses or bear the costs of unexpected care. The rest of us won't be able to recoup those losses if mistakes are made **unless we plan ahead**.*

Not Simply About Investing

Americans are by and large ill prepared for retirement. That's because the media, many of our financial institutions and even their own advisors have taught them to believe that retirement planning is simply about investing. It's not.

Retirement planning is about having a distribution strategy to make sure you don't run out of money before you run out of life. It incorporates pro-active, forward-looking tax planning and asset allocation, and takes into account all the risk management issues associated with retirement. For example, it's no secret that people are living longer than ever before, and this increased longevity provides an additional risk in our retirement planning. What were once viable income options, such as Social Security or pension plans, are no longer safe or realistic sole sources of income in retirement. A serious illness or premature death could also affect you and your surviving spouse's ability to continue to enjoy retirement.

Investments are merely tools for you to use unemotionally for securing your retirement dreams. It is the proper mix of these tools that will achieve the desired results for you, not a stock tip or a specific mutual fund. Assets are nothing more than future income streams consumed as needed. Proper planning should be viewed as a process, not as an event. As your life progresses and evolves, your planning will need to adapt to those changes. Health changes, marriage, divorce, retirement, death of a loved one and stock and bond market changes are all driving forces that require your plan to flex over time. In that respect, retirement planning is not dissimilar to a major horse race—the Kentucky Derby, for example. Each is about building endurance and stamina, about acquiring patience and possessing determination, about knowing the right time to surge and when to hold back, about being able to go the distance in order to cross the finish line—your retirement years—a winner.

DON'T TRIP UP!

Not planning or waiting until it is too late to plan are the most common mistakes retirees make. The power of compound interest is well known, but often ignored. Giving your savings the maximum amount of time to grow is your biggest ally.

Understanding the reality of how money works is crucial to a successful retirement. An analogy we like to use is the building of a house. A lumberyard supplies many of the products you need to build a home, but you probably would not go to the lumberyard to start designing your home. You should be just as careful in designing your financial home. Yes, of course, the products are important, but it's the design of the house that's key to aligning the suitable products and how to use them in the ways most beneficial to you.

Many consumers make the mistake of asking their financial advisors, "What product should I invest my money in?" Or "Where should I put my money?" These are actually the wrong questions to ask. Rather, they should be asking, "*How* should I be saving and investing my money?" This question acknowledges that the answer to building and protecting wealth does not lie in specific financial products you buy, but in how you *use* the various financial products in combination with each other. How your savings are invested is simply a by-product of your planning.

From the Horse's Mouth

Proper retirement planning is about getting the money you need in retirement out of all those places, such as a 401(k) or IRA, where you've been stockpiling it and into your hands in the most constructive and tax-efficient manner so that it will last as long as you do— and hopefully even longer for your family to enjoy.

The Components of Your Retirement Plan

The essence of a quality financial plan is that it allows you to see where you are today and what you envision for the rest of your life. Once you understand these two aspects, you can begin to bridge the gap between where you are and the goals you're trying to accomplish. Once you have your financial plan in place, seeing those goals next to your current financial picture may make you wonder whether or not they can be realized. The big question for us, as financial professionals, is whether and how the available assets can meet your future goals for you.

To determine the income you need now and also in the future, you need to view retirement planning from a liability standpoint. That means beginning with the guaranteed sources of income you have—Social Security, pension and annuity payments. The difference between that amount of income and what is needed is the deficit. You then need to allocate your savings to produce sufficient income to fill that deficit or "gap." That's your plan. If there are assets that won't be needed to fund your lifestyle now or in the future, then you can make arrangements in your plan to preserve and protect those dollars for the next generation in a tax-efficient manner.

FROM THE HORSE'S MOUTH

A deep and meaningful conversation with your spouse or significant other regarding what you really envision for your retirement and why you're doing the things you are doing will be paramount in crafting your overall written retirement income strategy. By understanding and living your life for the reasons that are important to you, and subsequently understanding what it takes financially in order to live your life this way, you can craft a financial plan that will be driven to allow you to live your life in the fashion that you see fit.

Creating a sound retirement plan depends on your fully understanding and working within the framework of the following components:

1. Your Current Financial Situation
2. Your Goals at Retirement
3. Resources for Achieving Your Goals
4. Outside Variables that Impact Goals

Let's take a look at them one at a time.

1. Your Current Financial Situation

We are all unique in our own financial situation. We each have specific spending patterns; some of us reward ourselves with buying goods/services, others can't spend a nickel without feeling guilt or fear. We were all taught certain views on money (our upbringing may still drive our current spending attitudes). We all view risk in very different ways; one person's view of a "conservative" investment might be very risky for others. Any type of planning should reflect your personal situation—but *especially* retirement planning.

Your *current financial situation* encompasses the following:

- *Current income (both spouses).* The total amount of your annual gross income, including salary, bonuses, and other sources of income.

- *Current expenses.* Your expenses for the past year (checking your bank statements will give you a good idea of where your money goes), including taxes (income and property), insurance payments, charitable giving, and other infrequent expenditures. Many times we look at our monthly or annual expenses and overlook items that come up only every few years but can be major budget items. Make sure you have really thought through all possible expenses in your future and have accounted for those consistently in a written retirement income strategy.

- *Current assets and liabilities.* Anything of value that you own—including certificates of deposit (CDs), bank accounts, stocks, mutual funds, cash, real estate, vehicles, jewelry, art, other collectibles, insurance policies and retirement accounts [IRA, 401(k), 403(b) and 457 plans]—are considered assets. Anything you owe—including a mortgage, credit card debt, auto loans, personal loans, 401(k) loans and margin balances in brokerage accounts—are considered your liabilities. *Your net worth is the amount you own less the amount you owe.* Always, always plan from a net perspective! Remember it's the net amount you can spend on a monthly basis that allows you to pay your bills, buy food, travel and all the other things you need in life. If you base your retirement plan on a gross income need, you won't be able to easily adjust your plan based on changes in the tax code. But if you plan for a net need you can easily adjust your plan and continue enjoying your retirement.

- **Current savings.** The number of dollars you are contributing each year to a retirement plan, including employer matching contributions, as well money deposited into a savings or brokerage account on a regular basis.

- **Employer-paid benefits.** Education reimbursement, paid time off, spousal benefits, discounts at various merchants, financial and personal counseling and any other benefits offered to you by your employer should be taken into account as part of current financial situation, as well.

2. *Your Goals at Retirement*

Ask yourself, "What would life be like if I had a strategy based on what is truly important to me where all the components of a well-crafted retirement income strategy are working in harmony with one another?" Not half-bad, right? In the grand scheme of things, money is not important. It is significant only to the extent that it allows you to enjoy what is important to you. By creating a written financial strategy that focuses on your life, your goals and the things that are important to you, you can begin to make intelligent decisions about the money that you accumulate and what it needs to do during your retirement years.

If you were to consult the best financial advisors on how to plan your future, they wouldn't start by educating you about market trends or mortality. They wouldn't try to explain the pros and cons of mutual funds, insurance or any other financial vehicle. And, they certainly wouldn't bore you with their resumes. Instead, they'd focus on what's important to *you*. Most retirement planning starts with an assessment of goals. But as important as these are, they don't provide you with the big picture—the *why* behind the rest of the plan. Goals are tangible results that you seek, while your values and what makes you excited to get up in the morning are the intangibles that make the pursuit of these goals genuinely meaningful to you.

Once you have clearly identified your goals, it's time to put a price tag on them. This process can be time-consuming, so be patient. Your money needs to work for YOU. In order to set your investments on the right track, you must truly identify what's important to YOU:

- *"What age do I want to retire?"*
- *"Will my spouse retire at the same time?"*
- *"What will I do with my free time?"* (Remember to factor hobbies into your income needs)
- *"How much net (spendable) income will I need every year?"* Always plan in net (after tax) dollars. As we've already noted, taxes will change in the future, so specifying a gross income need at retirement is simply not a safe and secure way to plan.

DON'T TRIP UP!

You've all heard about the purpose of diversification—to reduce risk. Yet many of you will have large percentages of your retirement funds concentrated in sector funds, company stock, real estate or a few stocks. You may be able to achieve spectacular results with concentrated investments but that is a strategy best left to investors trying to accumulate assets, not those trying to produce an income stream from those dollars. There is no shortage of horror stories (Enron, WorldCom, AIG) where employees and retirees lost much of their life savings when their company stock evaporated. Not being able to retire at the time and with the resources you had hoped for is not what you want happening to you.

3. *Resources for Achieving Your Goals*

You must take into account *all* of the resources available to you at retirement to help you reach your goals. Here is a partial list of them:

- **Social Security.** Social Security is in many cases the largest asset most people have in their retirement. But Social Security is a complex system that few people understand completely. There are many things to take into consideration, such as the taxation of benefits, reductions through early benefits, and break-even points. Think about it this way: In order for you to create the type of income that you would receive from Social Security, it would take a significant lump sum of money. Every individual in America who is eligible for Social Security is required under the current tax code to contribute 6.2% of every dollar they earn up to $106,200 and employers are required to match that dollar-for-dollar up to that same $106,200. If those assets were going into your 401(k) or IRA, more of you would pay attention to that account as a significant asset. Properly structuring Social Security can have a lasting impact on your long-term income needs. While the Social Security Administration can get you the basic numbers they really can't help you with how to effectively maximize your benefits. Survivor benefits, spousal benefits, penalties for filing early, and paying your benefits back are just a few of the issues you will face here. This is why we feel it is beneficial that you work with a financial advisor who clearly understands your needs and goals and how proper Social Security planning is necessary. This planner will help you run your complete plan with all the different possible scenarios as they relate to your Social Security income.

- **Pensions.** Although employer-sponsored pensions seem to be going by the wayside, many retiring employees will still have benefits to consider. There can be a whole host of options that you will need to evaluate, including whether to take a full lump sum, partial lump sum or income benefits. If you decide to take income benefits, do you need survivor benefits or can you maximize your pension benefits by incorporating life insurance? Do not make a decision without thoroughly evaluating each option—it can make a huge impact on your ability to reach your goals. Also, as some accounts are taxable, some tax-deferred and some are tax-free, the order in which you spend these accounts will have a dramatic effect on the success or failure of your retirement income. Run your plan and explore the difference to see which you should spend first and so on. There is no perfect order for everyone so this is something that has to be built in to YOUR written retirement income strategy.

- *Rental income.* If you currently own rental properties, will you be selling those at retirement or continuing to draw the income stream? Your decision will not only be financial, but could also depend on whether you want to continue owning and/or managing the properties.

- *Business sale/income.* If you own a business, will you be selling that business when you retire or continuing to draw income? If you plan on selling the business, do you know how much you will need to net from the sale? If you plan on continuing to own the business as you draw income, who will manage the business?

- *Part-time employment.* As a retiree, perhaps you would like to work at a library, garden nursery, woodworking shop or some other part-time job doing something you enjoy. Although you may think of the income as minimal, be sure to include it in your retirement plan.

- *Inheritance.* If it appears likely that you will receive an inheritance from someone at some time in the future, you will want to make sure that the inheritance will pass to you in the most advantageous way possible and that you consider the inheritance as potential assets in your retirement plan.

21

DON'T TRIP UP!

Relying on too few sources of income is a risk. Social Security, a pension and systematic withdrawals from savings might not be enough. Having multiple income streams that have the ability to offset the effects of inflation stacks the odds of a favorable retirement plan in your favor.

4. Outside Variables that Impact Goals

When you stop working, there are several things that may erode your money and your ability to have a successful retirement. Inflation will also slowly eat away at your savings—unless your retirement plan is designed to keep pace with it. But perhaps the least understood and most serious of these wealth-eroding forces is taxes.

Money can be taken away more easily than any other asset. Physical assets such as a painting, antique car, jewelry, collectibles, artifacts, land, or a home must be stolen or sold for you to lose them. But this is not true of money. You can lose a lot of money legally just from taxes, which is one of the most serious wealth-eroding forces you face.

The government uses tax revenue to operate, but our tax laws are constantly changing, so no one knows what the future tax laws will be. This undercuts the prevailing myth perpetuated by the business media and many in the financial services industry that when you retire you will probably be in a lower tax bracket than you are now. Take out the word "probably" and replace it with "unlikely" because any retirement plan predicated on the philosophy that taxes probably won't go up in the future may be invalid and unreliable. We are currently living with some of the lowest tax rates in history. To create your retirement plan with the assumption that these low taxes will last forever could be disastrous. This is why it is important to plan your goals on a net basis and consider the possibility of higher income taxes in the future. If you don't, you can lose significant amounts of money that you may never be able to recapture.

There are many income tax saving strategies to use. Tax *deferral* is one strategy. Many retirement savings plans today, such as the 401(k) and IRA, are tax-deferred, but this approach cannot win against taxes all by itself. It only delays taxation. In exchange for a tax break on your contributions, you must pay the piper eventually when you start withdrawing the money in retirement. By properly structuring your tax allocation strategy in retirement, you may improve your probability of success in cutting down and maybe even eliminating that bill.

FROM THE HORSE'S MOUTH

Municipal bonds can provide a stream of income free from federal, state and local taxes. Though many times the yields are lower than taxable investments, the tax-free effect can often make up for the difference in the stated yield. Through proper planning, you may actually end up with more dollars in your pocket. But beware. Beyond their tax efficiency, you should always look at the quality and chance of default risk of municipal bonds before choosing them for your retirement plan.

In addition to tax rates, another outside variable that can affect your retirement goals is inflation. Inflation is known as the "silent killer" in retirement because while many people have enough money to comfortably retire and get all the income they need in the first few years, the long-term impact of inflation on a successful retirement can be disastrous. We've all seen gas and food prices rise substantially over the past few years. Who knows how much they will grow up in the future. Inflation in retirement should be applied to various expenses differently, as opposed to lumping all expenses into the same category and applying the same inflation rate to all

HORSE SENSE

The very mention of the term "annuity" often brings fear to the heart of man (and woman). Without a doubt, it has to be the most misunderstood and unappreciated product available. This is not too surprising since there are so many different types of annuities and each has rules that are sometimes too complex even for trained agents and advisors to fathom. But with a knowledgeable advisor, annuities can potentially become a valuable part of your retirement strategy. The reason you should open your mind to this possible investment has to do with income growth and tax payment delays. Unlike other types of tax-deferred plans such as the 401(k) or IRA, which have contribution limits, there are no limits to how much you can put away for retirement in an annuity. The benefit base compounds year after year on a tax-deferred basis and you decide when to take taxable distributions. This can help you to be very tax-efficient and put you in control, rather than Uncle Sam. And finally, an annuity can serve as a complement to your Social Security, pension and other forms of retirement income. Before investing in any annuity, carefully consider the investment objectives, risks, charges and expenses of the annuity and its underlying investment options. The current contract prospectus and underlying fund prospectuses provide this and other important information.

of them. For example, if someone retires with a home mortgage of $1,500 per month and that loan will be paid off ten years into retirement, there is no reason to inflate that expense because it is fixed. But, if your health insurance costs $750 per month at the beginning of retirement, you may want to apply a 6% or 7% annual increase to this expense (the old average of 3% a year doesn't seem so reasonable anymore). So, your plan needs to be able to realistically address the "what if" factor of higher inflation on your ability to reach your goals. Itemize your expenses and determine which will inflate and which won't.

Here are more variables you should pay attention to:

- *Investment risk and returns.* If history is any guide it has shown us that over a long period of time, the equity markets typically go up, but in the short-term even history can't suggest what they'll do. As we learned in 2008, markets can take away much of the gains they have created in the blink of an eye. Imagine when you're retired if you see headlines about the market that aren't positive and you get a sinking feeling in the pit of your stomach as you wonder if you will be able to stay retired or have to go back to work. You may have to tell your spouse it's time to cut back and realign your retirement goals and expectations. Surely this is not what you had envisioned when you started planning. This is why it is absolutely critical that you know what your risk tolerance is and that you invest accordingly—though you may even find you need to take less risk than your maximum risk tolerance indicates. Stress testing your plan to make sure your portfolio can handle poor market conditions is necessary unless you live in a magical world where you can spend your gross income. You could use a tool called a Monte Carlo simulator that tracks your plan's progress, which takes into consideration the possibility of poor market conditions, and is stress tested to help you with proper asset allocation. In some cases, it may overstate the amount needed for a safe and secure retirement but we would rather you have too much than too little. Remember you can't spend average annual returns in retirement so don't plan your retirement income around them. It's not how much you make but how much you keep that allows you to have the income you need.

- *Pre-mature death of you or your spouse.* Death can be a tough subject to think about, especially your own. However, you need to make sure that your plan takes into account not only the unpleasant prospect of your untimely death but that of your spouse as well. This is because the passing of one spouse does not mean that living expenses of the surviving spouse automatically drop by 50%. They may remain the same—in which case the surviving spouse's income may not be sufficient. Mortality is 100% guaranteed, so it makes sense to plan for the possibility of a premature death. Ask yourself the question, "If my spouse or I die early what would change financially?" Be realistic and set contingency plans to mitigate financial loss.

- *Long-term care.* Advances in medical care have increased today's life expectancies substantially. One of the fastest growing segments of the population is the centenarian's. These advances have increased the chances that one spouse may become frail and need some form of care, which can be quite costly. Would you or your family be able to sustain an extra $10,000 to $12,000 monthly bill to care for you or your spouse at home? What would such an increase do to your retirement and legacy plans? Several years ago, a stroke may have meant certain death; today it may mean a few years' stay in a health care facility. Unfortunately, these facilities can be quite expensive, and if there is another spouse still living at home, the long-term care costs only add to the total household expenses. While some may say the perfect plan is to spend the last dollar on the day you take your last breath, others would likely rather have too much left over when they pass as opposed to running out and living 10 to 15 years beyond life expectancy. If your plan does not take you well beyond normal life expectancy, change the assumptions in your plan now!

All of these components need to be incorporated into your ongoing plan or the all-too-common result may be that you'll be missing out on the gold in those golden years.

Your goals may be entirely achievable given your current income, expenses and investments. You may already be on track. It's more likely, however, that you may have to make some adjustments in your approach:

- You can aspire to different goals. This is our second least favorite choice since goal reduction can be disheartening and demotivating.
- You can change your time horizon or your target date for achieving certain goals.
- You can increase your income. Like gas in the car, money fuels the plan so you can go the distance.
- You can adjust your expenses so you have more money to save and invest, thereby increasing your fuel another way. Some expenses are difficult to adjust because they have become part of your lifestyle. Others, such as taxes, you'd be happy to reduce (legally, of course).
- You can increase the rate of return on your investments. This is our least favorite choice because the pursuit of higher returns always means increased risk, and we have less control over return on investment than other options. Of course, it's the one many people like to tackle because it appears to be "easier." It doesn't require any personal discipline, like earning more money or adjusting your expenses. And if it doesn't work, many people shirk responsibility and blame their brokers or money managers. But any belief that you or anyone else can control or predict investment return or performance is an illusion.

Don't Trip Up!

Review your plan regularly. It will need adjustments over time. Debt, insurance, inflation, market movements, sources of income and family dynamics will always change. Protecting your nest egg with regular reviews is a must. It is imperative to adjust your allocations to ensure your strategy is the most advantageous as market conditions evolve.

Sequence of Returns

This "sequence of returns" concept is often overlooked in retirement planning decisions. We have divided retirees into two investor categories: Mr. Lump-Sum investor and Mr. Spender. The category you fall into is typically based on two factors: your current age and your financial goals. If you're Mr. Lump-Sum, this means you have a large sum of money that you leave untouched, or, in other words, you buy and hold. If you're Mr. Spender, you're most likely at retirement age and now dependent upon your accumulation for income.

To better understand the concept of "sequence of returns," consider the following scenario. Let's say Mr. Lump-Sum and Mr. Spender each have $100,000 in their respective portfolios at retirement. Mr. Lump-Sum leaves his $100,000 original investment untouched for ten years. But Mr. Spender begins withdrawing 6% (or $6,000) of his original capital at the end of the first year with 3½ % annual increases thereafter [for example, the second year withdrawal would be 6.21%, then 6.43% for the third year, and so on].

Now let's look at the "sequence of return" on four different portfolios over a ten-year period, as you can see in Figure 1. *These examples are hypothetical; they assume that initial and any future deposits and all withdrawals are made at the beginning and at the end of each calendar year, respectively. However, they do not assume the effect of taxes or fees. Annualized returns are computed using a time-weighted compound method.*

Portfolio A:	10	10	10	10	10	10	10	10	10	10	Average Return = 10%
Portfolio B:	-20	-10	-5	30	25	20	30	10	-5	25	Average Return = 10%
Portfolio C:	35	25	30	20	15	10	5	-8	-15	-17	Average Return = 10%
Portfolio D:	12	18	17	14	-8	-18	30	15	25	-25	Average Return = 8%

FIGURE 1

Now let's compare and contrast these differing portfolio results for Mr. Lump-Sum and Mr. Spender in Figure 2.

Portfolio A compounded at 10% each year for both retirees. For Portfolio B, the compounded rates of return are much different than the average rate of return. And for Portfolio C, the same differences occur between the average and the compounded returns. The differences in compounding for Portfolios A, B, and C are a result of the actual "sequence of return" and not the ten-year averages. What do we notice about the sequences? Portfolio A has no variability in annual sequence. Portfolio B has negative returns early in the sequence. And Portfolio C has negative returns late in the sequence.

What we see for Mr. Spender in Portfolio D is that it is possible to have an investment average of 8% return and finish with a higher value than a 10% average return due to "sequence of return" and cash-flow differences. This demonstrates that compounded rates of return are different than average rates of return, and that cash-flow behavior when combined with actual "sequence of returns" result in *actual investor return* that may differ from the actual *investment average return*.

	Portfolio A		Portfolio B		Portfolio C		Portfolio D	
	End Value	%	End Value	%	End Value	%	End Value	%
Mr. Lump-Sum	$259,374	10	$226,496	8.52	$226,951	8.54	$186,382	6.5
Mr. Spender	$150,161	10	$88,862	6.1	$161,203	10.58	$105,747	7.3

FIGURE 2

More Heads Are Better Than One

The financial markets around the world are more intertwined than ever due to the speed at which information travels. Plans must be able to adapt at the same speed. It is difficult enough to keep up with the necessary continuing education, rules, regulations and best practices for one niche area of planning, let alone the entire spectrum. That is why we recommend the use of experienced practitioners with qualifications in their area of specialty, who will encourage communication between you (the client) and each other to exchange ideas and develop a shared approach to customizing your financial plan.

We believe you should be completely free to concentrate on what is most important to you—living your life.

Like we always say, "It's not how much you make, but rather, how much you keep that counts." Integral to any plan is not only a good relationship between you and your financial advisor, but also a good and solid relationship between your financial advisor and your CPA, estate attorney, elder law attorney, insurance agent and so on. Having a team of professionals you can trust to give you the best advice and who are on the same page will help you develop a solid and proactive tax strategy. Remember though, a good advisor team and proactive tax strategy will only work if *you* act. But once you do, more benefits in the form of extra dollars will find their way into your pockets, both now and in the future.

The value-added of the team versus sole practitioner approach also extends to the staff that supports each advisor. A quality support staff enables advisors to spend all of their time and energy using their unique ability—helping clients achieve their goals and managing their plan. The old model of using a sole practitioner with a single support person forces advisors to spend too much time performing administrative work, not focusing on your retirement planning issues.

When scouting around for a planner consider these added benefits of choosing the person who is able to tell you that he or she is backed by a solid team of planning professionals to help navigate through the many services needed to meet your goals.

Teams can generate new energy. This energy evolves as team members fuse their individual strengths, reinforcing their separate capabilities and generating diverse ideas to deliver the best results for their clients. By bringing together experts with different skill sets, ideas and experiences, team members can develop options that come from discussion and debate. The magic happens when these skills and talents are brought together to blend with each other to find creative solutions to complex problems. When experts are allowed to stay closest to the work they know best, performance improves.

The bottom line: Take the time to learn the basics of retirement planning so that you'll know the right questions to ask, understand what the terminology means, and be able to recognize when something just doesn't seem quite right to you. Education will help you feel better about the choices you make and the people you hire to assist you in your planning efforts. Without confidence in your decisions, there is no peace of mind, only worry, which ultimately leads to poor decisions at the worst possible time.

There is no magic trick for escaping the simple facts of personal finance, unless you hit the jackpot in Vegas, win the lottery or receive some other financial windfall. Your retirement plan is about *planning* and not financial fantasy. It's where the rubber meets the road. So, consider where you are in each of the four quadrants of your plan. How much money do you have in cash reserves? Is your insurance sufficient? How much debt are you carrying in relation to your assets? These are known quantities. What remains is calculating the future, either through your own research or with the help of a professional. Now that you've prepared yourself, results will come from moving forward and actually taking action.

Don't accept any excuses!

NOTES

CHAPTER 2

THE STARTING GATE

Well, you did it—you've finally retired or are about to retire soon! Hooray! Now is the time to make some very important decisions about your finances, particularly that retirement nest egg in your IRA or company 401(k).

As professional financial advisors, we hear it all the time: "Come on, how hard can this really be? I have taken the time and spent the money to have my will drawn by the best attorney in town, I have trusts set up to avoid probate—I'm fine." Well, unfortunately, you're not....yet.

Although wills and trusts are fine and good, if you're like many people, your single biggest asset is your retirement plan. And, to give you a flavor for the kind of important information we'll be talking about in this book, that asset isn't passed on to your **heirs** (usually, your family, friends, or a charity) through a will or even a trust. Instead, it is passed by contract, according to your **beneficiary** designation form.

Often, the single most important estate planning move—making sure your plan beneficiary form is filled out correctly—is the most overlooked and yet the most important planning that you can do. We'll get into that in later in the book, and the advice you'll read there will save your family aggravation and maybe some green stuff too. We're hoping that you'll have money left when you pass away, money that you want to leave to your spouse, to your children, or your grandchildren. But keep something significant in mind: without proper planning, portions of the money that you worked so hard for over the years could go to the IRS instead of your heirs.

FROM THE HORSE'S MOUTH

Where do you want your extra money to go—to your family or to the IRS?

Now, that seems like a silly question, but, in reality, it is something all retirees must face. Why? Because most people don't know how to get their money to their heirs as they intended.

While retiring can be exciting, you also face the overwhelming chore of planning for the future. When it comes to your retirement plan money, you have three options:

1. You can stay put and leave your money in your company's plan. Relatedly, if you're changing jobs, you can even transfer your previous employer's retirement plan into your current employer's plan.
2. You can roll over your retirement plan money into an IRA.
3. You can take lump sum distributions.

1. Staying Put in Your Company's Retirement Plan

Due to convenience, many people keep their money exactly where it's always been during their working life: in their previous employer's retirement plan. Leaving your money in a company plan is sometimes the right decision—but sometimes it can be a sucker's bet. We see far too many people making this decision without knowing the full score.

It doesn't make sense to bet money on a horse that you know nothing about—unless you're dealing in pocket change you can afford to lose. When we're talking about retirement money, the stakes couldn't be higher. It's a race that we're sure you don't want to lose

Let's say that you are an employee who separates from service after age 55, but you're not yet age 59½. If you stay put, keeping your money in a company plan, you may access your funds penalty-free. If, instead, you had rolled over your funds into an IRA, and had not qualified for any of the special averaging techniques we'll discuss later, you would not be able to withdraw the funds penalty free from the IRA until reaching age 59½.

But this penalty is not the only consideration. Money that is left with an employer in any qualified plan is subject to more restrictive rules than money held in an IRA. For example, there are far more restrictions for your heirs if you pass away with money still in your company's retirement plan. We'll get into this more in Chapter 4.

Additional reasons for staying put and keeping money in a company plan include the ability to borrow against it and the opportunity to buy life insurance inside of the plan. Being able to buy life insurance within a plan can be a big advantage, because you cannot do that in an IRA. So, if you want life insurance and your company retirement plan allows it, but you aren't considered a top physical specimen for life insurance, if you're rated (you pay a higher premium due to health history or physical build) or if you are uninsurable, you'll want to stay put.

HORSE SENSE

If you need to stay with a company retirement plan for life insurance reasons, it may still be in your best interest to roll over SOME of your plan assets to an IRA. You will want to make sure that you keep enough money in the employer plan to pay for the life insurance.

A qualified advisor can help you figure out what insurance policies outside the plan are likely to cost, and whether it makes sense to consider such a strategy (see Chapter 7). Always consider what amount of life insurance your company's plan may allow you to purchase and what purchasing a comparable level of insurance individually will cost. If you are rolling out of a plan with life insurance and you want to maintain this insurance, make sure that your new life insurance policy is in force before any old coverage is cancelled.

If you are over age 70½, have money in a qualified retirement plan, *and are still working*, you may postpone required minimum distributions. Age 70½ is the "required beginning date" (RBD)—which is IRS jargon for the age at which you are required to begin minimum distributions, or taking money out of your plan. If this is your situation, and you don't yet need the money in your retirement plan, keep working and don't rollover your money to an IRA as long as you are still working.

For this "keep-working-and-don't-rollover" strategy to work:

- Your money has to be with the employer plan *where you are working*
- You must not be a 5%+ owner of the company
- The plan must allow postponing the required beginning date (many plans do not allow this!)

What if you already have an IRA, are approaching age 70½, and still working? See if your employer will allow you to roll over the pre-tax money from your IRA into the company's qualified plan. Not all company plans (especially if you work at a small company) allow this. If you have money in a plan with a former employer, and the employer will allow the transfer, complete a trustee-to-trustee transfer to your current employer's plan.

2. Roll Over to an IRA

The evidence overwhelmingly suggests that most employees and retirees are best served by rolling over their retirement plan money into an IRA. Let's take a look at why IRAs make sense, and how to best accomplish a successful rollover.

DON'T TRIP UP!

Keeping money in an employer plan where you work after age 70½ may allow for the postponement of your RBD, and/or allow for the ownership of life insurance. However, this strategy may still not be as advantageous for you as an IRA. Consult with a qualified advisor who can determine the best strategy given all the aspects of your current situation.

Many people want the ability to continue the tax deferral of their IRA as long as possible. A popular concept for doing this is called a "stretch" IRA (discussed in depth in Chapter 4). Retirees who choose to stay put with their company's plan, instead of going to an IRA, run the substantial risk of not being able to utilize the "stretch" concept. Here's why: if their spouse is their primary beneficiary, and the spouse dies before the account owner does, the bank or other custodian of the company plan is now required to allow a rollover to a non-spouse. This will instead force a lump sum distribution. As you'll learn when you read about "stretch" IRAs, lump sum distributions defeat the purpose of the "stretch" IRA.

Even if you're still working, and still contributing to your employer's plan, you may want to take out some plan money now and roll it over to an IRA. This is called an in-service withdrawal and not every plan allows this, but some of the larger employers will. The plans that I've seen allow in-service withdrawals after you have a certain number of years of service. They allow you to take a percentage of your balance out (they'll tell you how much). With this plan, you won't lose your eligibility for future company-matching, and your vesting schedule won't change.

There's one more reason to consider not staying put. In Chapter 6, we will discuss another type of popular investment account: the

Roth IRA. Current tax law allows IRA plan money and company plan money to be converted to a Roth.

Here are some key factors to consider when deciding whether or not to stay put:

- If you have health problems, and you have life insurance in your retirement plan, you should probably STAY PUT.
- If you may want a Roth IRA in the future, you may be better off NOT staying put.
- If you may want a tax-saving "stretch" IRA in the future, you may be better off NOT staying put.

IRA Rollovers (and Trustee-to-Trustee Transfers)

Most people don't stay put. They choose to roll over their retirement benefits outside of their company plan. The main reason they are advised to do this—and the reason it's usually the best choice—is *flexibility*. IRAs are more flexible both while you're alive and after you've passed away. The reason IRAs are more flexible is because most employers, whether they are a giant company or a small family-owned business, don't want to stay involved with employee's finances after retirement. Therefore, their qualified plans are designed to limit former employer's paperwork and logistical obligations.

For example, former employers don't want to be involved in the business of chasing down the beneficiaries of their deceased ex-employees. Because of this, their standard plan documents are set up to allow for a spousal rollover or a lump sum distribution. This means that the employee's family or the lawyer handling the estate will have to deal with notifying heirs, and former employers are off the hook.

Before we go deeper into IRA rollovers, we'd like to explain something that can be confusing. Technically, the term **rollover** means getting a check from your former employer and then, within 60 days, putting that money back into a qualified plan or an IRA. Another way to accomplish the exact same thing—without a check—is through something called a trustee-to-trustee transfer. Technically, a trustee-to-trustee transfer is not a rollover, though many people use these two terms interchangeably.

HORSE SENSE

An IRA offers far more choices to an individual than the typical employer plan. Even though employer qualified plans may offer as many choices as an IRA, for the reasons that we just discussed, employers who do not have to give you all the bells and whistles that an IRA can offer usually don't.

Have you quit your job, been downsized, laid off, or retired early? What are you going to do with the money in your retirement plan?

You could leave it where it is, transfer it to an IRA, or even take it as a lump sum in the form of a check. That last option sounds like fun. After all it's your hard-earned money, isn't it? The problem is, if you cash that check or don't roll it over into an IRA in your name within 60 days, the amount *becomes taxable*. Also, if you're under 55 when you separate from service, on top of the taxes owed, you will be hit with a 10% IRS penalty for taking the money out. This illustrates two of the most popular reasons why people roll over money in a former employer's plan to an IRA instead of simply cashing out: 1) to extend the tax deferral of retirement assets and 2) to avoid penalties.

What is tax deferral and why is it important? Tax deferral isn't the same thing as paying no taxes. What it does, instead, is delay the tax bill, allowing your money to grow without current taxation until a distribution is made from the account. In a qualified plan or an IRA, taxes are not due on earnings or growth until a withdrawal is taken.

If you have a large IRA balance ($300,000+ under current tax law), and choose to take a lump sum rather than roll over into an IRA, you're likely to pay handsomely to get that money in your hands. Assuming that you aren't eligible for any special averaging, you'll be hit with the highest federal income tax rate. (Be sure to read the lump sum distribution section at the end of this chapter to see if you're eligible for special averaging.)

Due to our progressive tax system, if you're not usually in the highest income tax bracket, biting the bullet and paying the taxes up front puts you at a tremendous disadvantage. Our tax system favors the taxpayer who can spread income over many years rather than those who must pay all at once. Relative to people with smaller IRAs, it'll take you some time just to recover the extra taxes that you have to pay.

That's like starting retirement with a financial handicap. Fortunately, this financial handicap can be avoided easily by steering clear of lump sum distributions that don't qualify for any of the tax breaks we'll discuss in length later.

Now, let's review the logistics of a rollover. If your employer hands you a check for your retirement benefits, you can cash the check and do what you'd like with the money. You might also consider a rollover: within 60 days, deposit the check back into an IRA, or into your new employers' qualified plan. Now, in the past, the IRS has granted some extensions to this 60-day rule but only in very limited circumstances, such as disability, hospitalization, when the post office loses your check, or in the case of an error by your previous employer's human resource department or financial institution. Don't count on the IRS granting an extension.

There are other potential problems with the rollover-by-check method. The federal government forces your employer to withhold 20% of the value of your retirement plan for federal income taxes when they perform a rollover. So, instead of the full amount, only 80% of your money is actually given to you. The government is concerned that you won't deposit all that money back into an IRA; they suspect that you might cash the check, spend all the money, and then be left unable to fully pay your income taxes and any potential penalties. Essentially, the government doesn't trust you with your own money.

DON'T TRIP UP!

The easiest way to avoid penalties, misunderstandings, and hassles is to never take a check from a former employer for qualified plan money. Instead, have your employer transfer your retirement dollars directly into your IRA. This is called a trustee-to-trustee transfer. Because you never physically touch the money, there is no risk of violating the 60-day rule.

Though you will technically get your 20% back when you file your federal income tax return, you have to be careful if you're under age 59½ and doing a rollover. Here's why: the 20% being withheld by your employer does not get rolled over by you, so you could be subject to the 10% early withdrawal penalty on those funds. This is in addition to any taxes that may have been triggered. Trustee-to-trustee transfers avoid the 10% penalty that the IRS slaps on taxpayers under age 59½ who receive lump sums.

HORSE SENSE

Here's another reason to avoid that pesky check, and instead complete a trust-to-trustee transfer. There is no limit to the number of trustee-to-trustee transfers you can do, which leaves you with more options and control.

IRA Advantages

What are some of the advantages the IRA has over a qualified retirement plan? Well, within an IRA, you have more investment choices than with an employer plan. With more opportunities, you are able to expand the ability to build an investment process to match your risk level and your income needs. In this business, we are fully aware that more choices can mean more confusion to some people. However, informed investors don't appreciate being limited to an employer's short list of investment choices.

DON'T TRIP UP!

If you have stock and cash in the company plan, your company may allow you to rollover stock "in kind." If you receive shares of stock from you employer's plan, you must deposit these shares into your IRA.

In other words, if you want to sell some or all of the assets from your previous employer's plan, you can do it and roll over the cash proceeds into the IRA. What the law prohibits you from doing is obtaining a stock certificate for the shares as you leave the plan, selling them, and then trying to deposit the cash in a tax-favored manner.

Need more reasons to consider an IRA? The second advantage of rolling over to an IRA, or performing a trustee-to-trustee transfer, is the ease of record keeping. You can consolidate multiple IRAs into one. We only recommend this move if it makes tax sense for you. Less paperwork is always good! And if you are your family's sole financial decision-maker, we encourage you to think ahead and reduce the paperwork burden on your family after you pass away. We'll revisit this topic later in more depth.

A third reason to favor an IRA is that as of 2010, non-spouse beneficiaries (children, significant others, grandchildren, siblings, etc.) can do direct transfers of inherited plan assets to an inherited IRA or convert them into an inherited Roth IRA. If you plan on leaving IRA money to a non-spouse beneficiary, be sure to read Chapter 4, which will go into detail about "stretch" IRAs.

Another important consideration that many people enjoy is the control that an IRA brings. If you have your own IRA, you are in complete control of your money. Want different investment choices than the ones that your employer offers? Then an IRA will be attractive to you.

Tired of having to call an 800 number and give a pin number to someone you have never met, who doesn't care about you, and doesn't have your family's best interests at heart? Then work with a local financial advisor—there are plenty of them all across the country, who, like us, have dedicated their professional lives to helping their own clients. We love getting your calls! And, after you pass away, your family can call someone they already know and trust, who has a secure relationship with the family's investments. It sure beats someone answering the phone at a call center who won't remember your name.

FROM THE HORSE'S MOUTH

The flexibility of an IRA can also make your estate planning significantly easier. Compared to a qualified retirement plan, IRAs streamline planning for primary and contingent beneficiaries. You'll also find that separating your IRA can be a useful advantage; you're allowed to split your IRA into multiple, smaller IRAs with different, distinct beneficiaries.

Lastly, an often overlooked advantage of the rollover is that you will then have the option of using the Roth IRA. Roth IRAs can be tremendous retirement planning tools. Chapter 6 is devoted entirely to the subject of the Roth IRAs.

3. Take a Lump Sum Distribution

We first discussed the option of staying put with your existing plan, then we explored the idea of rollovers and trustee-to-trustee transfers. Your third option is to take a lump sum distribution. That is, take out the entire dollar amount of your retirement plan and pay the taxes. This is the "take the money out, pay taxes, and be on your merry way" plan. You may need the money, you may just want to take the trip of a lifetime, or stick the money under your mattress. Whatever your plan for removing the money, you have the option of withdrawing a lump sum distribution from a qualified plan.

When they talk about lump sums, people usually mean removing *all* of your qualified plan money. But there's also a secondary option available: you can take some of the money out, and then roll over the remaining assets. Why would you pursue this option? Well, you might consider it if you were concerned with estate planning, and wanted to try balancing assets between yourself and your spouse to maximize your estate tax exemptions. If one spouse has the majority of the family's assets rather than an equal balance between husband and wife, she may take a distribution of some qualified plan assets and put the after-tax proceeds in her spouse's name.

Often, lump sums are eligible for some special tax treatments if you meet certain qualifications. There are a few situations where lump sum distributions can be especially attractive:

1. The first will apply a) if you hold stock in the company through your plan and b) if the stock has done well. Utilizing the Net Unrealized Appreciation (NUA) option will give you a tremendous tax break.

2. The second situation applies to younger retirees (under age 59½). Rule 72(t) (also called a series of substantially equal periodic payments) allows you avoid the usual penalties associated with removing qualified plan money before reaching age 59½. There are three different payout strategies allowed under 72(t), one of which may be attractive to you. See Chapter 3 for details.

3. Finally, if you were born before 1936, you are eligible for two special tax breaks. These are collectively referred to as the "special averaging method." The first benefit, called "ten-year averaging," applies only to those born prior to 1936. The second tax advantage is only available to those who contributed to their plan prior to 1974; under this rule, participants are eligible for an additional break referred to as the "20% capital gains treatment."

If any of these situations ring true for you, be sure to read Chapter 3, where we delve further into the details of these tax-advantaged strategies. Whether you choose to take advantage of ten-year averaging, a 72(t) schedule of payments, utilize the NUA of company stock, or use a twenty percent capital gains rate applied to pre-1974 plan contributions, there are a variety of different ways a lump sum can be developed to be most efficient from an income tax standpoint.

You May Want to Consider a Lump Sum Distribution if:
- You are eligible for lump sum tax advantages (as explained above)
- For estate planning purposes, you maintain a goal of balancing assets
- Your distribution is small, and will not cause you to be bumped into a higher income tax bracket
- You think that a) someday down the road you'll be in higher tax bracket than the one you're in on the day you retire, and b) feel paying taxes today, at that lower rate, is beneficial— terrific!

Is My IRA Safe from Creditors?

The enactment of the "Bankruptcy Abuse and Consumer Protection Act of 2005" (called BACPA for short), makes IRAs more attractive than ever. Before this act, some investors were reluctant to convert qualified plans to IRAs because, in a few states, assets held in an IRA didn't come with the same protection from creditors that assets held in retirement plans enjoyed. BAPA created a broad new federal exemption for tax-qualified retirement benefits reserved for instances when the account owner must file for bankruptcy. This new exemption eliminates many of the distinctions that once helped creditors seize debtors' retirement plans. The new exemption applies to IRAs, 457 plans and 403(b) plans, in addition to traditional company sponsored plans.

This decision greatly improves the protection of IRAs but it is limited exclusively to Bankruptcy Court, and does not apply in all courts. You must investigate your state's own bankruptcy exemptions, since some states do not allow for the use of federal exemptions or will force the debtor to choose between the state and federal regulations. For example, in New York State, the New York Debtor and Creditor Law, Section 284, prohibits a debtor from using the exemptions in the Federal Bankruptcy Code. But, New York also provides more protection to IRAs than the federal laws.

At the same time that a debtor is most vulnerable and seeking bankruptcy protection, creditors will often take advantage of all opportunities to prove that a retirement plan doesn't meet *each* requirement of the tax code. Unfortunately, creditors often succeed. Be careful! Hire expert counsel in bankruptcy law if you must file for bankruptcy while you hold assets in a retirement plan.

Hopefully, this chapter provided you with an understanding of the options you have for moving retirement plan money into an IRA. The rest of the book is dedicated to helping you figure out which strategies are right for you, your retirement plan and your IRA.

NOTES

CHAPTER 3

THREE WINNERS IN THE DISTRIBUTION RACE

Have you ever attended a sporting event that you didn't under-stand? When you're a rookie—new to racing—you probably arrive for the day without even having read about the ponies running in the day's events. At the track, you take a long look at the regulars who are engrossed in sizing up the field and weighing everything they've ever learned about racing before they enter a single bet. That's when the rookies begin to wonder, "What do they know that I don't?"

The same is true when it comes to deciding how to take money out of retirement plans and IRAs. In Chapter 5, entitled "Cashing Out," we'll discuss this topic in depth. Here, however, we're talk-ing about some special rules that won't apply to most people. In the retirement plan distribution world, you can play by special rules and get special tax breaks if any of these situations describes you:

1. You own highly appreciated company stock in a qualified plan.
2. You are a (lucky!) young retiree under age 59½.
3. You were born before 1936.
4. You were born before 1936 AND contributed to your com-pany's retirement plan before 1974.

Do you have highly appreciated, publicly traded company stock in your qualified retirement plan? **Highly appreciated stock** is stock that was acquired at a much lower price than it is selling for now. Often, if you've worked for the same employer for many years, you do. The term *net unrealized appreciation* is more IRS jargon that describes a particular situation: you withdraw your company stock from your company retirement plan which you don't rollover. Instead, you actually take the stock out of the plan, but in lieu of paying ordinary income tax on the fair market value, you pay it on your *cost basis*. This is a much lower number if your stock has done well!

FROM THE HORSE'S MOUTH

NUA stands for Net Unrealized Appreciation and is one of the most underused assets within a company plan. It is the difference in value between the average cost basis of shares of stock held in a tax-deferred account and the current market value of those shares. It can become very important if you are distributing highly appreciated company stock from your tax-deferred company plan such as your 401(k). Upon distribution, the NUA is not subject to ordinary income tax. For this reason, it may be better to separate the NUA from the 401(k) rollover by placing it into a regular brokerage account. Otherwise, if you roll it over, it eventually will be taxed at your ordinary income tax rate upon distribution.

To qualify for NUA, you must first take a full distribution of your retirement plan. In addition to the stock, if you have any mutual funds or money market balances, they must also come out of the plan. Those non-stock assets should be rolled over into your IRA or another qualified retirement plan, or moved using a trustee-to-trustee transfer before you take your distribution of stock. By doing this, the funds in this particular transfer will not be taxable. Only the withdrawal of the company stock creates a taxable event. Remember that you are not obligated to withdraw 100% of your company stock. All, or part, of your company stock can be withdrawn with any remaining shares rolled over or transferred to an IRA. You only pay ordinary income tax on the shares not rolled over, because those shares are included in your gross income.

Here's a quick example: John is retiring at age 60. He's planning to take a lump sum distribution from his retirement plan, where he has 10,000 shares of company stock in his plan. His cost basis is $5/share and the fair market value is $35/share. John will receive a 1099R from his company indicating a gross distribution of $350,000 (10,000 shares at $35/share). The 1099R will also show a taxable amount of $50,000. This is the taxable amount that John's income taxes will be based on (10,000 shares at $5 cost basis). His NUA is $300,000. If John immediately sold his stock at current market rates, he would gross $350,000, and would have to pay long-term capital gain taxes on the $300,000 of his NUA.

Another example: Instead of immediately selling his stock, John waits three months after he retires. By this point, his stock is now worth $45/share, which influences John's decision to sell all of his stock. The numbers in this case work out the same as those in the previous example: $300,000 NUA with $50,000 taxed at the ordinary income tax bracket. But now, because the stock has appreciated to $45/share, John has a short term capital gain of $10/share because the stock has not been held for 12 months since being distributed. That $100,000 is the appreciation between the date of distribution and the date of the sale of the stock. So, in addition to his long-term capital gain of $300,000 on his NUA, John also has a short term gain of $100,000 on the appreciation since the distribution date.

Given this information, what if John waited one year from the date of his distribution to sell his stock? Regardless of the price, all gains would be long-term capital gains, because he has waited the requisite full year.

51

So how do you determine the amount of your NUA? First, your employer is supposed to quantify how much of a distribution of the company's stock constitutes NUA. This taxable figure is then reported on 1099R form (in box 6). You'll want to know this amount no later than when you are taking your distribution. You don't want to wait until January of the following year when you receive the 1099R and find that the number is wildly different from your anticipated figure.

Suggestion: Stocks which you hold outside of a qualified plan come with a built in advantage your heirs will appreciate. When you die, they will enjoy what is called a **stepped-up basis**. This means that the cost of the shares is determined to be the market value of the shares on the day that you died, regardless of what your cost basis was. It is important for you to know this. After you perform the NUA distribution calculations, you might decide, "Oh, I am never going to sell it." However, when you take this employer plan stock to your grave, and haven't yet sold the shares, the IRS's rule is that your stock will not receive a step up in basis. What happens? The NUA that you received when you took distribution of the stock retains its character as NUA after you die.

Your beneficiaries will receive the same tax treatment that you would have, had you lived and sold the stock yourself. Unless the stock appreciated in value, from the time that it was distributed until the time that you died, your beneficiaries will fair no differently. This portion of the appreciation does receive favorable tax-treatment, though. When your heirs sell that stock, this extra appreciation will be added to their cost basis.

Let's try to translate this by example. In the case of John, his original cost basis is $50,000, and his stock was worth $350,000 at the time it was distributed. John never sold any of his shares during his lifetime. John's beneficiaries will then continue to receive the same tax treatments as he did. So if they sell the stock after John dies, and it is still worth $350,000, John's heirs will owe long-term capital gains on the NUA of $300,000. But what if John's stock had appreciated to be worth $500,000 at the time of his death? His heirs would still have long-term capital gains on $300,000 of NUA, but they will receive a stepped-up basis from the $350,000 GE was worth at distribution to the $500,000 at the date of John's death. In other words, they pay no taxes on those $150,000 of the gain.

Now, what if John's heirs do not immediately sell any stock after John passes away? They continue to hold it and the shares appreciate to $600,000. His heirs will still owe the long-term capital gains on the $300,000 original NUA, plus capital gains on the additional $100,000 in appreciation since John passed away. That additional $100,000 in appreciation could either be taxed at short-term or long-term rates, depending on how much time has elapsed.

NUA Accounting Tips

NUA Accounting Tip #1: To avoid a tricky situation where your employer withholds 20% of your distribution, make sure your employer first sends any non-stock assets you had in your plan (i.e., your mutual funds or money market accounts) directly to the custodian of your IRA via a trustee-to-trustee transfer. Again, trustee-to-trustee-transfers require no withholding by your employer. Once this is done, your NUA shares can be distributed with nothing left in your company plan for the IRS to withhold.

NUA Accounting Tip #2: Don't wait until the very end of the year to take your stock distribution. Your employer may need a few weeks to process the distribution, and for an NUA transaction to be allowed, the entire distribution must happen within one calendar year. Don't wait until the last minute and get burned by a slow response from your human resources department. Remember to keep your NUA stocks separate from other company stock you may own. Stow them in a separate account so your record keeping won't be complicated. You don't want to go through the effort of an NUA transaction only to have it ruined by poor record keeping that threatens your claim to a tax break.

NUA Accounting Tip #3: Start planning your NUA transaction early in the year and get your basis in your stock from your employer. They are required to provide it for you, so if you run into some red tape, don't back down.

We'll share a real life example: one of us recently met with a client who was terminally ill. His beneficiaries were his two daughters. Like many folks, he kept his retirement money with his employer long after retirement. While planning his estate, however, he ran into a problem—the employer's plan design would not allow his daughters to stretch his retirement money over their lifetimes. Compounded with this catch, he also had highly appreciated employer stock. So, after weighing our options, we rolled his non-stock company plan assets (cash and fund balances) into an IRA and made his daughters the beneficiaries of his IRA. This was not a taxable event, and it was done with a trustee-to-trustee transfer. The children now have the option to stretch the distributions of their father's IRA over their entire lifetimes.

Next, we took a distribution of his employer stock, with its built-in NUA, which allowed his daughters to sell the stock whenever they choose and pay only the capital gains rate on the sale. If the client had died without taking the distribution of this employer stock, distributions from his IRA would be taxed as ordinary income, not as capital gains.

FROM THE HORSE'S MOUTH

If you're in a similar situation— with a non-spouse beneficiary and highly appreciated stock—think ahead. Non-spouse beneficiaries can also utilize NUA, but they can now also do the direct transfer to an inverted IRA.

NUA Planning Tips to Get Lower Tax Rates

NUA Planning Tip #1: How does a gift for the grandkids straight from Uncle Sam's pocket sound? We thought you'd like that idea! With the 0% capital gains tax rate currently in place for the lowest income earners, think about gifting some of your NUA stock to your grandchildren, who are probably in a lower bracket. They, in turn, can sell the stock at the 5% rate on the untaxed appreciation.

NUA Planning Tip #2: If you are thinking long-term, keep in mind that, in 2008-2012, the tax rate on qualified dividends and long term capital gains is 0% for those in the 10% and 15% income tax brackets. After 2012, dividends will be taxed at the taxpayer's ordinary income tax rate, regardless of his or her tax bracket. After 2012, the long-term capital gains tax rate will be 20% (10% for taxpayers in the 15% tax bracket). After 2012, the qualified five-year 18% capital gains rate (8% for taxpayers in the 15% tax bracket) will be reinstated.

NUA Planning Tip #3: You don't give up your rights or flexibility by performing an NUA transaction. Owners of NUA stock still retain all the rights and options that any shareholder enjoys. If you wanted to diversify your holdings, for example, you always retain the option to sell the stock, pay a capital gains tax and reinvest your proceeds. Another option is to contribute your stock to a charitable remainder trust. We'll discuss that in Chapter 4.

Useful in some high net worth situations, you might also consider performing an NUA transaction followed by placing the stock in an **exchange fund**. (An exchange fund is a vehicle that enables an investor to contribute concentrated positions of low-basis or restricted shares in exchange for shares in a professionally managed, diversified investment portfolio). Exchange funds can be very sophisticated instruments, however, with requirement details beyond the scope of this book. Consult your personal advisor if you feel this might be a worthy investment for your assets.

A perfectly planned NUA transaction will take into account tax deadlines, which allows an investor to delay when taxes are due. We prefer to see our clients complete the distribution in year one, paying the ordinary income tax when it is due, and then postpone the capital gains tax on the stock they want to sell until the next calendar year. Staggering the transactions may prove to be very useful for your tax planning.

DON'T TRIP UP!

There are situations when not deferring tax on your NUA might work and even make more sense. Why? If you qualify, you may be able to have the entire value of the stock taxed using ten-year averaging. If your company stock has not appreciated, or you do not have a large distribution, you may actually pay less tax using the ten-year averaging method, which is described later in this chapter.

In the case of **Private Letter Ruling** (a regulation drafted by the IRS in response to an appeal for clarification or a ruling by a taxpayer) number 200442032, a taxpayer lost the benefit of Net Unrealized Appreciation on his employer's stock in his qualified retirement plan when the stock was *mistakenly* rolled over to an IRA. The IRS refused to permit the taxpayer to rescind the rollover. Here's what

happened: The taxpayer was retiring from his job. He had participated in his company's retirement plan and all his holdings were his
employer's stock. Prior to retiring, he met with his financial advisor;
they decided to take a lump sum distribution of his stock which was
eligible for the tax advantage of net unrealized appreciation.

After opening an account to accept the stock, the taxpayer asked
how the account should be titled. The financial advisor told him to title the account as "Custodian C, for [taxpayer's name] benefit, IRA."
After receiving this advice, the taxpayer contacted the employer's
human resource department to initiate the distribution. During his
conversation with HR, the taxpayer was told that a transfer to an IRA
is irrevocable. He acknowledged this, and told the employer to transfer his stock to his account, which was titled as the financial advisor
had indicated. Two days later, the financial advisor realized his error,
and the taxpayer and his advisor contacted the employer to attempt
to stop the transfer into the account titled as an IRA. The employer
indicated that it was too late to change, and the shares were subsequently transferred into the IRA account. The taxpayer requested
that the IRS permit him to personally revoke the rollover, and treat
the stock as if it had been directly transferred to the taxpayer.

The IRS denied his request. As a result, any distributions from
the IRA are subject to ordinary income taxes. What a clear example
of bad advice causing harm! Reminder: you cannot rely on another
taxpayer's Private Letter Ruling to protect your actions. It applies
only to that particular taxpayer.

Series of Substantially Equal Periodic Payments—72(t)

If you are under the age of 59½ and you want to take money
out of your retirement account, the IRS will penalize you 10%
for taking what the IRS likes to call a "premature distribution."
This section of the IRS code is called 72(t), and was added by the
Tax Reform Act of 1986. 72(t) has gone through several versions
thanks to amendments over the past two decades. This 10% penalty is viewed by the IRS as a way to encourage you to save money
not only for retirement but also *until* retirement, which they continue to define as age 59½. 72(t) is essentially tax jargon for a rule

that allows investors to avoid the 10% penalty if they withdraw retirement plan money before they reach the federally regulated retirement age. Rule 72(t) is often referred to as a **series of substantially equal periodic payments**.

HORSE SENSE: 72(T) FACTS

• *The 10% IRS penalty is calculated only on the part of the distribution that is included in your gross income.*

• *Withdrawing company stock for NUA after age 55 will not trigger the 10% penalty.*

• *Distributions that include basis will pay the same penalty but only on that part which is included in gross income.*

• *Rollovers and trustee-to-trustee transfer are not included in gross income.*

Let's be clear on this: You may be able to avoid a financial penalty using 72(t), but you'll still pay normal taxes. So, even if you avoid the penalty, you are still going to owe the IRS income taxes. Therefore, investors should take into account the possibility of depleting their retirement account well before the end of their life expectancy.

To qualify for 72(t), your distribution must be either a) at least over a five year period or b) until you reach age 59½, whichever takes longer. The five year period closes at the end of the five years beginning with the distribution, not on the date of the last distribution (see: Arnold v. Commissioner, TC No. 12 (1998)). This series of periodic payments is sometimes called annuitizing, which should not be confused with buying an annuity.

The payout amount is determined by your life expectancy, according to the IRS actuarial tables. Once you begin the payments, if you make a change and take either more or less than your scheduled payment, you'll pay dearly. The IRS calls this "modifying" the payment schedule. You are not only hit with a 10% early withdrawal penalty on distributions taken prior to age 59½, retroactive from day one, but the IRS will also charge you interest on top of the steep penalty.

Usually, 72(t) payments must be at least made annually. They must also start after you have separated from service (when you no longer work for that particular employer), unless your employer's plan permits called in-service withdrawals. These allow employees to rollover a portion of their plan to an IRA. Then a series of substantially equal periodic payments can begin from the IRA.

IRS Revenue Ruling 2002-62 and Notice 89-25 are the official guidelines for determining acceptable methods for taking periodic payments. The goal of these strategies is to determine the largest payments possible using the smallest amount of money from the IRA. This will leave more of the IRA balance intact and accumulating tax-deferred money.

Utilizing 72(t) for one IRA has no impact on any other IRAs you own. So, once you determine how much of a withdrawal you will need to make each year, you should calculate how much of your IRA will be needed to fund these payments. If this calculated dollar amount is less than the total value of all your IRAs, you should split them. This way, the remaining balance won't be affected by your payment schedule. If more cash is needed, you can always start another 72(t) schedule with another IRA. You only want to annuitize the amount of your IRA that you will need to satisfy the imposed payment schedule.

72(t) Tips

- Payments that are part of a series of substantially equal periodic payments are not allowed to be rolled over to another IRA. If you do not need the entire amount of each payment, reinvest the remainder into a taxable account.
- Periodic payments are also exempt from the mandatory income tax withholding rules for distributions from qualified retirement plans.
- The mandatory withholding rules only apply to distributions that are eligible for a rollover.

Payment Calculations Under 72(t)

There are three different methods for determining your payment schedule under 72(t). The **minimum distribution method** is the first method under 72(t). Payments are determined in the same manner as required minimum distributions are calculated once you reach age 70½. Your annual account balance as of December 31st of the previous year, or a balance on a date which the IRS deems a "reasonable period," is divided by your life expectancy every year to determine your payment. The definition of a "reasonable period" is not clear but the most widely used method of determining that period is a date between the date of your first payment and December 31st of the prior year. If your first distribution will be on June 1, it would be reasonable to choose an account balance on any day between December 31st of the previous year and June 1.

Of the three available methods for calculating a series of substantially equal periodic payments, this method will produce the smallest payment. These payments will oscillate depending on fluctuations in the value of your account each year. As the account grows, the payment will increase, and vice versa, which will cause a certain amount of unpredictability in your cash flow.

Let's look at an example: You retire at age 52 with a $100,000 balance in your IRA on December 31st, and you need to take distributions. During year one, you will look up your life expectancy factor from one of the three IRA life expectancy tables. For the purposes of this example, we will choose the single life table, which yields a factor of 32.3 years. To calculate, divide your balance of $100,000 on December 31st by your life expectancy factor of 32.3 to determine your first annual periodic payment of $3,096. This is the amount that you must take out of your IRA, using the minimum distribution method, to avoid penalties.

In year two, you will perform the same process. Assume that the balance of your IRA on December 31st has grown to $105,000 due to investment performance. You will again look up your life expectancy, this time as a 53 year-old, which yields a factor of 31.4. Divide $105,000 by 31.4 to determine your second year payment of $3,344. You should continue this process until you reach age 59½.

Are you wondering why your life expectancy was 32.3 years at age 52, and, one year later, it is 31.4 years (but not 31.3 years)? Life expectancy is a moving number; the older you are, the longer that you are expected to live!

The **amortization method** is the second method available for determining a payment schedule under 72(t). With this method, you will choose an interest rate to amortize your account balance. The interest rate you may use is defined by the IRS as "an interest rate not more than 120% of the Federal mid term rate in either of the two months prior to the first distribution." Information on this rate is available at the IRS web site, www.irs.gov. The rate is subject to change every month, but you won't have to refigure your calculation every month. When running your numbers, you will use the "annual" interest rate because your payments must be made at least annually. You'll then look up your life expectancy and account balance (just as you would for the minimum distribution method) and *amortize* your account, using the interest rate that you chose over your life expectancy.

To amortize means to come up with a series of payments. There are multiple software programs available that will do this for you and most financial institutions are equipped to help. You can double check the accuracy by computing the payment using a financial function calculator, such as Hewlett Packard's HP-12C. You compute the payment as you would a mortgage payment using your account balance as the amount, your life expectancy as the number of years to repay the loan and the interest rate you have chosen as the borrowing cost.

Let's review another example. Your account balance is $100,000 when you begin taking distributions at age 52. You choose to use 4.5% as your interest rate. Your life expectancy from the single life table is 32.3. You calculate the payment as amortizing the $100,000 over 32.3 years at 4.5%. Your required withdrawals will be $5,931/year.

Think of this method as your mortgage payment in reverse. This will be your fixed annual payment every year you continue with your series of substantially equal periodic payments. This method provides more certainty of cash flow, especially when compared to the required minimum distribution method. After year one, the IRS allows a one time change in payment method to the required minimum distribution calculation, for the amortization and annuitization methods only.

The third 72(t) payment option is the **annuitization method**. Again, you choose a reasonable interest rate, determine your account balance, and find your annuity factor. The annuity factor is based on certain interest rate and mortality assumptions used mostly by actuaries. With this information, you then divide your account balance by your annuity factor (which will depend on your age and the interest rate you have chosen). Determining your annuity factor is different than determining your life expectancy. Unfortunately, the IRS has not computed these factors for us but there are multiple software programs available to help. The IRS has stated that using this method "generally requires professional assistance." This means you'll most likely want a professional to assist with any calculations, and help you pick an appropriate interest rate. Like the amortization method, this annuitization method will yield equal payments every year. You can also elect to change your calculation method to the required minimum distribution method after year one. And, like the amortization method, only one change is allowed.

Let's look at an example of the annuitization method. An IRA owner has a $100,000 balance when distributions begin at age 52, with a 4.5% interest rate. Using software programs available today, he determines that the applicable annuity factor is 17.021. He then divides the $100,000 balance by the applicable annuity factor, 17.021, to determine that each and every year's payment will be $5,875.

Record Keeping

The IRS released a Private Letter Ruling that decided in favor of a particular taxpayer because of his diligent record keeping. The taxpayer had established a 72(t) schedule using the amortization method. All went well until the IRA custodian screwed up and did not send the required payment in December. Rather, it arrived in January. The financial advisor noticed the final distribution was not made on time and requested a "make up" payment which was sent in January. Since the taxpayer didn't get 12 monthly payments by the end of the year, the IRS considered the payment schedule modified and assessed a 10% penalty under Code section 72(t)(1).

The taxpayer, however, requested a ruling that the failure to take the December payment was not his fault. He had submitted the necessary paperwork and did all he could in order to ensure that he would receive the balance of the annual payment on time. He stated that he had no reason to believe the IRA custodian would not make the distribution as requested. Moreover, the taxpayer did not intend to modify the series. Because of these factors, the IRS ruled that the missed payment and subsequent "make up" distribution was not considered a modification of the series, and therefore withdrew the 10% penalty.

72(t) Accounting Tip

Depending on how the form 1099-R is coded when you receive it from the IRA custodian, you may need to file additional paperwork. If 1099-R box 7 is coded with a 2 (early distribution, exception applies under age 59½) then no additional forms need to be filed. If box 7 has a code of 1 (early distribution, no known exception) or 7 (normal distribution) that means the IRS doesn't recognize that you are taking a tax-favored 72(t). In this case, you must file IRS Form 5329 to claim the exemption to the 10% penalty tax.

Choosing a 72(t) Method

- The **minimum distribution method** is the easiest and simplest method to understand, but it does have some drawbacks. With fluctuating payments, the minimum distribution method does not offer a predictable cash flow.
- With the **amortization method**, payments are fixed. However, the calculation for determining payments is comprehensive and complex, and the IRS has the power to disallow the amortization method if you do not follow

it completely. Also, with this method, your payments will be slightly higher than the required minimum distribution method.

- With the **annuitization method**, you will have the ease of fixed payments and the flexibility to choose your interest rate, capped at 120% of the federal mid-term rate in either of the two months prior to the first distribution. This will ultimately determine your annuity factor. The higher the interest rate, the bigger your payments. Remember, don't be too aggressive, or the IRS could disqualify your payment schedule.

HORSE SENSE

Mistakes can cost you dearly. Be conservative in your estimates. The longer you establish the time frame for your series of payments, the more conservative you may want to be. For example, the 72(t)tax break could be disallowed if you choose too high an interest rate (which will make your payments too high). Learn the rules and then hire someone to help you so you don't become a 72(t) horror story in a future book!

Thoughts on 72(t)

Revenue Ruling 2002-62 states that the required minimum distribution and amortization method requires you to use one of three established life expectancy tables for calculating payments. These include the single life, joint survivor, and uniform lifetime tables. We cannot recommend any one method over another—you should consult with a CPA and financial advisor who are well versed in 72(t) payments and utilize the available software programs to assist you with your decision. Each situation is different and requires gathering and analyzing available information.

Who is 72(t) right for? If you retire before you reach age 59½, your IRA probably represents your largest asset, and includes the finances you need to live on. If you are 55 or older when you retire, you can also take money from your company plan penalty free. But if this is not an option, roll it to an IRA. Even if your qualified retirement plan allows 72(t), the IRA is more attractive because it is flexible and allows you to split your money into multiple IRAs.

If you are involved in a divorce, and need to make alimony payments before you reach age 59½, using 72(t) could result in a better deal than choosing to transfer a portion of your IRA directly to an ex-spouse. This way, you won't be considered to have modified the payments.

Advanced 72(t) Planning

Consider a well-to-do couple where one spouse holds most of the family's financial assets in her IRA. In this case, trying to equalize the ownership of financial assets can be difficult. A planning technique that works well is to take 72(t) payments and use distributions to fund a taxable account in the name of the spouse who doesn't own the IRA. This is especially attractive when you are trying to build your spouse's estate to utilize the federal estate exemption. Remember, with the federal estate exemption, you either use it or you lose it. You do have the option to take the payments, which can fund life insurance premiums owned outside the estate, which will then pay estate taxes to keep the IRA intact for the next generation.

What does the IRS consider modification to a payment schedule? If you fail to take a payment or take an extra payment it won't fly with the IRS. We know what you're thinking: "Hey, if I take an extra payment, that'll create more revenue for the IRS, so they won't care! I'll just take one extra payment." It's not worth it—taking the extra payment is considered a modification. Just a reminder: when the IRS says you've modified a payment schedule, you're going to pay penalties.

Exceptions to the Penalty:

- Both death and disability (but only total disability where you are unable to work in any substantial gainful activity) are considered exceptions by the IRS. To claim either a physical or mental disability, you have to be able to prove your case to be one of indefinite duration.
- Plan-only distributions under a qualified domestic relations order are exempt.
- If you are unemployed, you could take IRA-only penalty-free distributions for health insurance premiums and higher education costs (including tuition, fees, and books at an eligible education institution), and medical expenses in excess of 7½% of your AGI from both plans and IRAs, including reservist plans and IRAs.
- The IRA-only first time home purchase exception allows up to $10,000 dollars for you, your spouse, your children's, or your grandchildren's home purchase.

These are a few ways you can avoid the stiff penalties. Otherwise, make sure to seek the guidance of a financial advisor to skip the sticky situations.

Ten-Year Averaging

In addition to NUA and 72(t) payments, there is one other special tax break, called **ten-year averaging**. This incentive is only available to those born prior to year 1936. If your lump sum distribution meets certain requirements, you will receive tax breaks. With this break, the IRA allows you to use 1986 tax rates to pay taxes on your distributions, as if they were ten small distributions rather than a single, larger distribution paid in one year. However, the tax payment is not spread out. Despite the 10 year tax calculation, you pay the total tax due when you pay taxes for the year of the distribution, not over 10 years. Even though tax rates were higher in 1986 than they are today, your overall tax burden can be reduced using this strategy.

FROM THE HORSE'S MOUTH . . . .

When you pass away, your beneficiaries can use this ten-year averaging policy, if you would have qualified.

Ten-year averaging is a once in a lifetime choice. Once you choose this distribution method, you may not use it again for any future distribution from any plan. If you have multiple retirement plans and you receive distributions from more than one in a single year, you must use ten-year averaging on all distributions you receive that year.

Are You Eligible for Ten-Year Averaging?

- You must be born before 1936.
- The distribution must come from a qualified retirement plan, not an IRA.
- The distribution must consist of your entire plan balance, minus any voluntary contributions (the amount that you contributed).
- Your distribution must come out in one taxable year.
- You must have been a participant in the plan for at least five years.
- And you should investigate Form 4972, which can be used as an official checklist to determine all ten-year averaging qualifications.

Now on to the hows and whys of ten-year averaging. The ten-year averaging tax is considered separate from your regular income taxes, so your adjusted gross income is not increased by your distribution. You don't lose deductions, you don't lose credits, and you will not trigger the alternative minimum tax. Ten-year averaging will not affect the taxation of your Social Security payments.

HORSE SENSE

If you have a lump sum worth less than $70,000, you are also allowed to exclude a portion of the tax due from the ten-year calculation. This is called the minimum distribution allowance. It is deducted from the dollar amount of the taxes due.

The lure of paying less money in taxes through ten-year averaging is easy to understand but it will come at the expense of future compounded growth in your retirement plan. The tax advantages of ten-year averaging diminish as the amount of your distribution increases.

Let's see an example: a $100,000 distribution using averaging will result in slightly less than 15% due in taxes—$14,470. Using the 1986 tax rates, the tax rate increases substantially when dealing with higher dollar amounts. A $600,000 distribution results in a tax bill of $187,386, a 31% tax bracket. That may or may not make ten-year averaging a bargain. You'll want to do your homework prior to electing ten-year averaging. It may not be the best alternative, especially if your retirement plan value is substantial. So, depending on your income, the current marginal tax rates, and the amount of money in your company retirement plan, ten-year averaging can be either a winning strategy or a clunker.

Ten-year averaging and pre-1974 plan participation strategies are found in IRS Form 4972. The capital gain portion of your distribution will be shown in box 3 of Form 1099-R.

Here are some significant examples of ten-year averaging and utilizing capital gain treatment reporting: Robert Smith was born

DON'T TRIP UP!

Beyond ten-year averaging, if you were a participant in a qualified retirement plan prior to 1974, and if you were born before 1936, you could also elect to use a flat 20% capital gains tax rate on the portion of the lump sum distribution you contributed prior to 1974. This 20% rate is fixed, regardless of the actual capital gains tax rates currently in effect. So, when you are dealing with smaller dollar amounts for pre-1974 money eligible for the 20% rate, you may actually be better off from a tax point-of-view skipping the ten-year method. Remember to run the calculation both ways before making a decision.

in 1935 and retired from Crabtree Corporation in 2004. He chose to withdraw the entire amount of his retirement plan. In 2004, he received a total distribution of $175,000. Of the $175,000, $25,000 consisted of his own employee contributions, and $150,000 was a combination of employer contributions and earnings on all contributions.

Robert receives a 1099-R showing the capital gain portion of the distribution to be $10,000. He elects the 20% capital gain treatment on this portion. He enters the capital gain of $10,000 on Form 4972, Part II, line 6 and the capital gains tax of $2,000 ($10,000 distribution times 20% tax rate) on Part II, line 7.

He has $140,000 of ordinary income from the distribution and elects to use ten-year averaging. He enters $140,000 on Form 4972, Part III, line 8. The tax of $24,270 is reported on line 43 of his Form 1040.

Here is what Robert's 1099-R and 4972 would look like:

☐ CORRECTED (if checked)		
PAYER'S name, street address, city, state, and ZIP code Crabtree Corporation Employees' Pension Plan 1111 Main Street. Anytown, Texas 75000	**1** Gross distribution $ 175000.00 **2a** Taxable amount $ 150000.00	OMB No. 1545-0119 2010 Form **1099-R**	**Distributions From Pensions, Annuities, Retirement or Profit-Sharing Plans, IRAs, Insurance Contracts, etc.**
	2b Taxable amount not determined ☐	Total distribution ☒	**Copy B** Report this
PAYER'S Federal identification number 10-0000000	RECIPIENT'S identification number 002-00-3456	**3** Capital gain (included in box 2a) $ 10000.00	**4** Federal income tax withheld $ 30000.00	income on your Federal tax return. If this form shows Federal income
RECIPIENT'S name Robert C. Smith		**5** Employee contributions or insurance premiums $ 25000.00	**6** Net unrealized appreciation in employer's securities $	tax withheld in box 4, attach this copy to your return.
Street address (including apt. no.) 911 Mill Way		**7** Distribution code(s) IRA/SEP/SIMPLE 7A ☐	**8** Other $ %	This information is being furnished to
City, state, and ZIP code Anytown, Texas 75000		**9a** Your percentage of total distribution %	**9b** Total employee contributions $	the Internal Revenue Service.
Account number (optional)		**10** State tax withheld $ $	**11** State/Payer's state no.	**12** State distribution $ $
		13 Local tax withheld $ $	**14** Name of locality	**15** Local distribution $ $
Form **1099-R**			Department of the Treasury - Internal Revenue Service

Form **4972**	**Tax on Lump-Sum Distributions**	OMB No. 1545-0193
Department of the Treasury Internal Revenue Service (99)	(From Qualified Plans of Participants Born Before January 2, 1936) ▶ Attach to Form 1040 or Form 1041.	**2010** Attachment Sequence No. **28**

Name of recipient of distribution	Identifying number
Robert C. Smith	002-00-3456

Part I   Complete this part to see if you can use Form 4972

			Yes	No
1	Was this a distribution of a plan participant's entire balance (excluding deductible voluntary employee contributions and certain forfeited amounts) from all of an employer's qualified plans of one kind (pension, profit-sharing, or stock bonus)? If "No," **do not** use this form	1	✓	
2	Did you roll over any part of the distribution? If "Yes," **do not** use this form	2		✓
3	Was this distribution paid to you as a beneficiary of a plan participant who was born before January 2, 1936?	3		✓
4	Were you (a) a plan participant who received this distribution, (b) born before January 2, 1936, and (c) a participant in the plan for at least 5 years before the year of the distribution?	4	✓	
	If you answered "No" to both questions 3 and 4, **do not** use this form.			
5a	Did you use Form 4972 after 1986 for a previous distribution from your own plan? If "Yes," **do not** use this form for a 2004 distribution from your own plan	5a		✓
b	If you are receiving this distribution as a beneficiary of a plan participant who died, did you use Form 4972 for a previous distribution received for that participant after 1986? If "Yes," **do not** use the form for this distribution	5b		

Part II   Complete this part to choose the 20% capital gain election (see instructions)

6	Capital gain part from Form 1099-R, box 3	6	10,000
7	Multiply line 6 by 20% (.20) . . . . ▶	7	2,000
	If you also choose to use Part III, go to line 8. Otherwise, include the amount from line 7 in the total on Form 1040, line 43, or Form 1041, Schedule G, line 1b, whichever applies.		

Part III   Complete this part to choose the 10-year tax option (see instructions)

8	Ordinary income from Form 1099-R, box 2a minus box 3. If you did not complete Part II, enter the taxable amount from Form 1099-R, box 2a	8	140,000
9	Death benefit exclusion for a beneficiary of a plan participant who died before August 21, 1996	9	
10	Total taxable amount. Subtract line 9 from line 8	10	140,000
11	Current actuarial value of annuity from Form 1099-R, box 8. If none, enter -0-	11	-0-
12	Adjusted total taxable amount. Add lines 10 and 11. If this amount is $70,000 or more, skip lines 13 through 16, enter this amount on line 17, and go to line 18	12	140,000
13	Multiply line 12 by 50% (.50), but do not enter more than $10,000 . **13**		
14	Subtract $20,000 from line 12. If line 12 is $20,000 or less, enter -0- **14**		
15	Multiply line 14 by 20% (.20) **15**		
16	Minimum distribution allowance. Subtract line 15 from line 13	16	
17	Subtract line 16 from line 12	17	140,000
18	Federal estate tax attributable to lump-sum distribution	18	
19	Subtract line 18 from line 17. If line 11 is zero, skip lines 20 through 22 and go to line 23 . .	19	140,000
20	Divide line 11 by line 12 and enter the result as a decimal (rounded to at least three places) . . . . **20** .		
21	Multiply line 16 by the decimal on line 20 . . . . **21**		
22	Subtract line 21 from line 11 . . . . **22**		
23	Multiply line 19 by 10% (.10)	23	14,000
24	Tax on amount on line 23. Use the Tax Rate Schedule in the instructions	24	2,227
25	Multiply line 24 by ten (10). If line 11 is zero, skip lines 26 through 28, enter this amount on line 29, and go to line 30	25	22,270
26	Multiply line 22 by 10% (.10) **26**		
27	Tax on amount on line 26. Use the Tax Rate Schedule in the Instructions **27**		
28	Multiply line 27 by ten (10)	28	
29	Subtract line 28 from line 25. Multiple recipients, see instructions . . . . ▶	29	22,270
30	Tax on lump-sum distribution. Add lines 7 and 29. Also include this amount in the total on Form 1040, line 43, or Form 1041, Schedule G, line 1b, whichever applies . . . . . . ▶	30	24,270

For Paperwork Reduction Act Notice, see instructions.	Cat. No. 13187U	Form **4972** (2010)

Form 4972 Tax on Lump-Sum Distributions 2010. Summary: This is an example of Form 4972 (2009) with items included as described in the text. Additionally, these line items are also completed:

Under "Name of recipient of distribution" field contains **Robert C. Smith**
Under "Identifying number" field contains **002–00–3456**

Under "Part I: Complete this part to see if you can use Form 4972":

"1. Was this a distribution of a plan participant's entire balance (excluding deductible voluntary employee contributions and certain forfeited amounts) from all of an employer's qualified plans of one kind (pension, profit-sharing, or stock bonus)? If No, do not use this form. YES" **checkbox checked**

"2. Did you roll over any part of the distribution? If Yes, do not use this form. NO" **checkbox checked**

"3. Was this distribution paid to you as a beneficiary of a plan participant who was born before 1936? NO" **checkbox checked**

"4. Were you (a) a plan participant who received this distribution, (b) born before 1936, and (c) a participant in the plan for at least 5 years before the year of the distribution? YES" **checkbox checked**

"5a. Did you use Form 4972 after 1986 for a previous distribution from your own plan? If Yes, do not use this form for a 2002 distribution from your own plan. NO" **checkbox checked**

Under "Part II: Complete this part to choose the 20% capital gain election (see instructions)":

"6. Capital gain part from Form 1099-R, box 3" field contains **10,000**

"7. Multiply line 6 by 20% (.20)" field contains **2,000**

72

Under "Part III: Complete this part to choose the 10-year tax option (see instructions)":

"8. Ordinary income from Form 1099-R, box 2a minus box 3. If you did not complete Part II, enter the taxable amount from Form 1099-R, box 2a" field contains **140,000**

"10. Total taxable amount. Subtract line 9 from line 8" field contains **140,000**

"11. Current actuarial value of annuity from Form 1099-R, box 8. If none, enter 0" field contains **0**

"12. Adjusted total taxable amount. Add lines 10 and 11. If this amount is $70,000 or more, skip lines 13 through 16, enter this amount on line 17, and go to line 18" field contains **140,000**

"17. Subtract line 16 from line 12" field contains **140,000**

"19. Subtract line 18 from line 17. If line 11 is zero, skip lines 20 through 22 and go to line 23" field contains **140,000**

"23. Multiply line 19 by 10% (.10)" field contains **14,000**

"24. Tax on amount on line 23. Use the Tax Rate Schedule in the instructions" field contains **2,227**

"25. Multiply line 24 by ten (10). If line 11 is zero, skip lines 26 through 28, enter this amount on line 29, and go to line 30" field contains **22,270**

"29. Subtract line 28 from line 25. (Multiple recipients, see instructions)" field contains **22,270**

"30. Tax on lump-sum distribution. Add lines 7 and 29. Also include this amount in the total on Form 1040, line 42, or Form 1041, Schedule G, line 1b, whichever applies" field contains **24,270**

TAX ON VARIOUS LUMP SUM DISTRIBUTIONS

If Your Lump Sum Distribution Is	10 Year Average Tax[1] is:
$ 100,000	$ 14,471
150,000	24,570
200,000	36,922
250,000	50,770
275,000	58,270
300,000	66,330
318,833	72,733
350,000	83,602
375,000	93,102
400,000	102,602
450,000	122,682
500,000	143,682
550,000	164,682
600,000	187,368
650,000	211,368
700,000	235,368
750,000	259,368
800,000	283,368
850,000	307,368
900,000	332,210
1,000,000	382,210

[1] Based on 1986 tax tables

When you take a distribution from a retirement plan, the custodian (or the institution that holds your account) issues an IRS Form 1099-R to both you and the IRS. You are not required to attach this form to your tax return unless income tax was withheld from your distribution. If tax was withheld, you must attach a 1099-R to your return when filing to show how much was withheld.

If you were under 59½ when you took the distribution, in box 7 of 1099-R the number "1" should appear. This indicates that the early distribution tax applies in your case. If you are under age 59½ but you qualify for an exception to this tax, box 7 should reflect this.

Box 7 Exception Codes:

- "3" indicates a disability exception
- "4" is a post-death distribution
- "2" is for most other exceptions

HORSE SENSE

When it comes to taking your money out of a qualified plan, don't think that all your options are mutually exclusive. Sometimes the winning ticket is to take some money out under one particular option, and take the rest out under another option or two. For example, if your retirement plan consists of mutual funds, money market deposits, and company stock, and you take a full lump sum distribution, you may be able to take advantage of three tax-saving strategies: deferring taxes using NUA, using ten-year averaging for non-stock assets and you might even qualify for the 20% capital gains treatment.

Even if you are eligible for one of the tax-saving strategies discussed in this chapter, you will still want to read Chapters 4 and 5. Remember, you can take a strategy from this chapter, then "stretch" some money, and even distribute some the old fashioned way.

NOTES

CHAPTER 4

DOWN THE "STRETCH"

The term "stretch" IRA has become very popular over the last few years. The "stretch" IRA is not a product. Rather, it is a process that allows for tax deferral to continue beyond the lifetime of the IRA owner. While a Roth IRA offers tax-free growth, a traditional IRA offers tax-deferred growth. That's it! That is the big secret of the "stretch" IRA, the dynasty IRA, the legacy IRA, or the multi-generational IRA—or any other name that you've seen to describe the concept. It boils down to this: after the IRA owner dies, the retirement account keeps growing on a tax-advantaged basis for the beneficiary who inherited it—for as long as the law will allow. The "stretch" IRA tends to work very well for retirees who don't think they'll ever need all their IRA money; or for the beneficiary of an IRA. (If you inherit IRA money, you will need to know what steps to take, and what deadlines exist, when the IRA owner dies).

The latest change to the tax code supports the stretch IRA strategy. The new code requires smaller amounts to be forced out of retirement accounts after age 70½ by way of required minimum distributions, which leaves a larger portion of your principal intact for your beneficiaries. If you don't plan to spend your entire retirement account balance, you might as well learn the most efficient way to get it to your beneficiaries rather than just giving a chunk to Uncle Sam when you die. So, the real question is: how do you stretch?

HORSE SENSE:

1. Make sure you use an IRA custodian which will allow you to stretch (not all do!).

2. If you have money in a qualified retirement plan, get it out and rollover to an IRA.

3. Name a designated beneficiary on your IRA beneficiary form. If you haven't named a designated beneficiary, the custodian will usually force a lump sum distribution. A designated beneficiary must be a living person or a trust that qualifies as a designated beneficiary.

If you have designated a beneficiary, he will be allowed to stretch the post-death required minimum distributions over his life expectancy (according the IRS Single Lifetime Table). Later in this chapter we'll discuss what happens when a beneficiary has not been designated.

This "stretch" can be maintained even after the primary beneficiary dies. If the beneficiary of the inherited IRA dies before his or her actuarial life expectancy, the successor beneficiary of the IRA can continue to take the required minimum distributions for the remaining time left on the original beneficiary schedule—instead of the typical five-year payout. It's as simple as that. With a "stretch" IRA, we are able to keep our money tax-deferred (through an IRA), or tax-free (with a Roth IRA) over multiple generations.

DON'T TRIP UP!
. . . .

The IRS spelled out that every single inherited IRA and inherited Roth IRA can now be stretched. Stress the term IRA and Roth IRA! Not every retirement plan will qualify to be stretched out—only those. Qualified retirement plans are not required to allow for stretching room. The IRS will allow a stretch concept in a qualified retirement plan, but the plan documents must provide for it, and many employers' plan documents do not. As we said at the beginning of the book, most employers do not want the workload or the liability of continuing correspondence with their deceased ex-employees' beneficiaries over the next 50, 60 or 70 years. It's as simple as that.

Why does stretching work? Because we as taxpayers are faced with a **progressive tax system**, in which high income taxpayers usually pay a higher tax rate than low income taxpayers. Therefore, spreading out any taxes due over longer periods of time rather than paying all at once almost always decreases the rate at which taxes are paid. Another way to diminish taxes is by spreading a dollar of tax liability over more than one tax return (by designating multiple IRA beneficiaries). Meanwhile, until the balance is exhausted, the IRA has the potential to grow without current taxation, and the earnings are **compounding** which means they're staying put, generating earnings on earnings. This is the beauty of the "stretch" IRA—a powerful tool that can be used to build wealth.

The "stretch" concept also applies to Roth IRAs, which can provide tax-free growth, instead of tax deferred expansion. Remember that distributions to beneficiaries come out of a Roth IRA tax-free, as long as they are **qualified distributions**. For more information on Roth distributions, be sure to read Chapter 6.

Let's put the "stretch" concept of a Roth IRA into perspective. The current IRA contribution limit is $4,000 per person per year. Thus, if a twenty year-old begins making annual $4,000 contributions for the next 45 years, and is able to compound those contributions at an 8% annual earnings rate, when he retires at age 65 he will have accumulated over $1.54 million. That is just the mathematics of it! Investing $4,000 per year for 45 years at 8% equals $1.54 million!

Now, what if, instead of starting with a $4,000 IRA balance, your 20 year-old daughter creates her retirement savings with a $400,000 IRA balance which she inherited from your estate? That $400,000 sum will compound over her lifetime with a "stretch" IRA. The resulting dollar amount is staggering. You may have seen these charts, and you may have thought that the numbers shown seemed ridiculously high. Whenever we look at one of these charts with a client, we inevitably get the same response: "Yeah, it looks good on paper, but the required minimum distributions will stop that growth from happening in the real world." Sounds too good to be true? Let's do the math.

While planning your estate, you chose to leave your IRA to your daughter, who is now 50 years old. She will have to withdraw that money at a starting rate of approximately 3% because of her age. So if the account balance is earning more than a 3% rate of return, the account has to grow. Again, it's simple mathematics. The higher the rate of return over the rate of the distribution, the more the account is going to grow. Let's take it a step further.

Let's say that, instead of leaving your IRA to your successful 50 year-old daughter, you instead leave it to your 18 year-old grand-daughter. At her age, your granddaughter is only required to take approximately 1.5% of the account value for required minimum distributions. Now, keep in mind, she can always take more. But, remember, we are talking about trying to stretch it for as long as possible.

You may say, well, 1.5% doesn't matter very much. However, we have participated in situations with clients where the beneficiary is a college student. Her parents understand that a little extra cash can go a long way, so we give a little latitude towards extra distributions. When the beneficiary needs money the most, whether it is now or in college (or when she is out of school and into her first job, or is busy raising a family—whatever the case may be) the beneficiary can always take out more than the required minimum

DON'T TRIP UP!

Try and preserve the stretch by not taking more than the growth of the account. We're not saying you shouldn't ever touch the principal; but to maximize stretch benefits, try to avoid raiding the account. You'll thank us later!

distribution. One well received idea is to withdraw more than the Required Mimimum Distribution (RMD see Chapter 5), maybe the amount of growth in the account, every single year. This will bring more money to the beneficiary whenever it is needed.

Multiple Beneficiaries

What if the "stretch" concept seems attractive but you have more than one beneficiary? In the case of an IRA owner who has four children, there can still only be *one* designated beneficiary per retirement account for distribution calculations. However, what will happen if you list your four children, with equal proceeds going to each? The eldest child, who also has the shortest life expectancy, will be the one automatically considered the designated beneficiary. The oldest child's life expectancy is what will be used to calculate the amount of required minimum distributions that have to come out of the inherited IRA.

Often, in the case of multiple children, their ages are relatively close together, because they were usually born within a few years of each other. When this is the case, using the oldest child's divisor does not make a significant difference. But sometimes this doesn't hold true. If, for example, there are more than ten years between you and your sibling, this can add up to a big difference when figuring IRA distributions. When you have multiple beneficiaries on one IRA, the oldest child—who is the oldest beneficiary—uses his divisor to determine the minimum distributions for all the other beneficiaries. But when you have a later discrepancy in age, the younger beneficiaries get the short end of the stick. Younger beneficiaries are allowed to withdraw much smaller amounts from inherited IRAs, maximizing the tax-advantaged stretch.

This consequence of beneficiaries with large age differences becomes a bigger problem when we are not talking solely about children as beneficiaries. What if the IRA owner names his brother, age 75, along with his 40 year-old daughter, as beneficiaries? Does the same situation occur? If they are both listed on the IRA beneficiary designation form, they will each get a 50% share as equal beneficiaries. The required minimum distribution on an inherited IRA is going to be based on Uncle Ralph's life expectancy, which for a 75 year-old is 13.4 years.

Your daughter, who could have taken the money out over her 38.8 year life expectancy, is now losing out on twenty five years of tax advantages because of the way that the beneficiaries were named. Because the difference between these two ages is so significant, the daughter's distributions will be very negatively impacted. She's stuck with Uncle Ralph's life expectancy to determine the required minimum distributions from the IRA.

Separating IRAs

How can this unsatisfactory outcome be avoided? Are there other options? Let's say that you are the IRA owner, and you leave your $500,000 IRA to Uncle Ralph and your daughter, by designating them both as beneficiaries. Each of them will get a 50/50 stake. Based on Uncle Ralph's life expectancy of 13.4 years, the required minimum distribution on the $500,000 account value divided by his 13.4 year life expectancy is $37,313 for this year's required minimum distribution. Because they are co-beneficiaries, they will split this figure between themselves.

However, if instead of sharing the IRA with Ralph, your daughter had her own IRA, she would able to use her own life expectancy factor (a much plumper 38.8 years). Her required minimum distribution would only be $12,887. Look at the difference between these two numbers: nearly $25,000. Your daughter's RMD would obviously be lower because she could stretch her IRA much longer. Remember, if your daughter's life expectancy is used (which won't happen if she inherits an IRA with an older co-beneficiary), she will always have the option to take a higher distribution.

The IRS allows you to split an IRA into as many separate, smaller IRAs as you chose. Therefore, in the example of Uncle Ralph and his niece, instead we can split the $500,000 IRA into two $250,000 IRAs. That gives the daughter far more choices, and certainly doesn't hurt Uncle Ralph's investment. If a case with three multi-aged beneficiaries, we would probably want to make a similar move and turn one IRA into three individual accounts. Do note, though, that you can't split an ordinary qualified plan—this is an IRA-only benefit!

DON'T TRIP UP!

The IRS allows IRAs to be split post-death; even after the IRA owner passes away; his beneficiaries may choose a smarter route and spilt their assets. Splitting IRAs must be done as plan-to-plan transfers, meaning they are not taxable events. Everything still stays sheltered under the traditional or Roth IRA umbrella and can be split after a death.

Splitting the IRAs involves a limited window of time. You have until December 31st of the year following the IRA owner's death to split accounts. That said, we strongly suggest completing the split by September 30th. Remember Murphy's Law—you don't want to jeopardize the stretch by waiting until the last minute, especially if RMDs are due.

This period of time between the death of the IRA owner and September 30th of the following calendar year is known as the "shake out period." This time frame can be as short as one year and one day (if death occurred on December 31st) or as long as one year and 364 days (death occurred on January 1st).

This time is available so that involved parties can assess who the beneficiaries are and what action should be taken for each. During this time, some decisions need to be made. They may include some of the following questions: Are the IRA assets needed to pay any estate tax? How should each beneficiary receive their share of the IRA? Young beneficiaries may want to explore the stretch concept. Wealthy beneficiaries may choose to disclaim or give back their share. Beneficiaries being hounded by creditors or perhaps involved in a messy divorce may choose to disclaim to avoid an inheritance leaving the family. Beneficiaries who are not *designated* beneficiaries should be paid their share quickly or have their share split into a separate IRA to ensure the stretch concept for any of the designated beneficiaries.

Skillful planning at this juncture can be the ultimate determinant as to how the IRA owner's wishes and beneficiary's needs are best addressed. Let's go back to the previous example: Uncle Ralph will inherit 50% of the IRA, as will your daughter, though her share will be nestled into her own separate, inherited IRA. Now, each beneficiary will be able to use his or her own life expectancy to compute the required minimum distribution.

However, let's use this information to create at a new example: John Smith, our IRA owner, dies in 2004 at age 75. His two children and a granddaughter are his IRA beneficiaries. His son is 49 years old, his daughter is 46, and his granddaughter is 15 in 2005. John designated each of his children to receive a 40% share of his IRA and left a 20% share to his granddaughter. John's IRA balance on December 31, 2004 was $500,000. He had already taken his required minimum distribution the year he passed away.

If John did not split the IRA, and his beneficiaries were unaware that they had such an option, the situation would play out in a particular way. The three beneficiaries would be required to use John's eldest son's life expectancy; for a 49 year-old, this equals 35.1 years. This figure poses no real problem for John's daughter, who is fairly close in age with her brother. Unfortunately, John's granddaughter will lose most of the benefit of stretching the IRA. Instead of being able to stretch her share over her 67.9 year life expectancy, she is stuck with her uncle's. The granddaughter's required minimum distribution is going to be much higher than it could have been, and the duration of her payouts are almost half what they would have been using her life expectancy factor. So in 2005, John's granddaughter's share of the $100,000 investment, divided by her uncle's life expectancy is $2,849. Remember, she can always take more, but her required minimum is much higher than it would be using her own figures.

Using the same example, we can see the differences if John had split his IRA into three separate accounts for his beneficiaries. John's children would each walk away with a separate IRA worth $200,000, and his granddaughter would have $100,000 in her own inherited IRA. Because she will be able to use her own life expectancy of 67.9 years, John's granddaughter's required minimum distribution will drop down to $1,473 in 2005. That is roughly half of what she would be required to take under the first scenario, when she was forced to use an inappropriate life expectancy. In addition, once the IRAs are split, if his granddaughter were to die at unexpectedly at age 45 (30 years from now), her beneficiary could then continue the required minimum distribution on her original schedule. In other words, her beneficiaries would have another 37.9 years to stretch the original inherited IRA. As soon as IRAs are split, the new owners should each immediately name their personal beneficiaries.

Don't Trip Up!

Distributions from inherited IRAs (called a death distribution) avoid the 10% early withdrawal penalty for any beneficiary under the age of 59½.

Titling an Inherited IRA

When IRAs are split, it's important to make sure they are titled correctly. An incorrectly titled account may allow the IRS to force a total liquidation, with large consequences—removing the entire benefit of the stretch.

To continue with our most recent example, John Smith's beneficiaries should title their accounts as follows. For his son: John Smith IRA, Deceased July 1, 2004, FBO Bob Smith, beneficiary. For his daughter, the IRA should be titled: John Smith IRA, Deceased July 1, 2004, FBO Sue Smith, beneficiary. And his granddaughter's account should read: John Smith IRA, Deceased July 1, 2004 FBO Emma Smith, beneficiary. The IRS has not issued official instruction on how to title accounts, and it's up to you, through proper titling, to make it clear that it is an inherited IRA.

HORSE SENSE

The example above may sound redundant, but we wanted to make sure we drilled it in. The correct titling makes a clear message to the IRS: the rights to the IRA belong to the beneficiary, but it is still the decedent's IRA.

The beneficiary cannot make contributions to the inherited IRA, but the beneficiary's social security number is listed on the account. Why? Because, at the end of the day, when distributions come out, the beneficiary has to report those distributions as income (and incur a taxable event if the inherited IRA is a traditional IRA).

Recently, more and more IRA providers have begun using new forms when an IRA is inherited. The new form, or account agreement, allows the beneficiary to name his or her own beneficiaries. What if your beneficiaries are not all designated beneficiaries? Let's say that you want to name a child as one beneficiary and a non-person as another—such as your estate or a charity. This gets a little tricky. Your IRA may be split prior to your death (or by December 31st) to ensure the designated beneficiary—in this case, the child—will qualify for the benefit of the stretch. As mentioned earlier in this chapter, we always recommend splitting the IRA sooner rather than later. Beneficiaries are often slow to act after the loss of a loved one, and time is of the essence when dealing with a split.

If the account beneficiaries don't act in time to split the accounts, the child will lose the benefits of a stretch. Using the previous example, where multiple beneficiaries were all individually designated beneficiaries, the IRA could still stretch if it hadn't been split. This would take place over the lifetime of the oldest beneficiary. When one of the beneficiaries is not the designated beneficiary, the charity, estate or other like-beneficiaries do not have a life expectancy. Thus, they cannot allow for a stretch. Therefore, when you have a beneficiary listed who is not a designated beneficiary, it becomes much more important to split the accounts ahead of time, or make sure it is done by September 30 of the following year after the IRA owner's death. This way, the designated beneficiary still receives the option to stretch.

We are often asked, "How long can I really stretch an IRA?" The answer is that the IRS will not allow a beneficiary to stretch an IRA longer than his own life expectancy. A newborn has an 82.4 year life expectancy. Accordingly, this is the maximum stretch on an inherited IRA. But let's look a little closer. We want to give you the true flavor of how long an IRA can really "live" or stretch. Imagine that you (as IRA owner) contributed for 50 years while you were working, and then, for twenty years after retirement, you took distributions. When you passed away, your wife rolled your IRA over, treating it as her own, and she took distributions for another ten years. She designated your granddaughter as beneficiary, so when your wife passed away, the account went directly to your granddaughter. Your granddaughter keeps it as an inherited IRA and took the required minimum distributions over her lifetime. In this situation, the IRA actually lived a great deal longer than 82.4 years. An IRA has the great potential to grow well beyond the lives of you and your spouse, and through the life expectancy of your designated beneficiaries.

Death of the Beneficiary

What happens to an inherited IRA when the beneficiary dies? When a beneficiary dies (let's call him Beneficiary One) while receiving distributions, the beneficiary's beneficiary (let's call her Beneficiary Two) receives the remaining IRA distributions on the timetable of Beneficiary One's life expectancy. The new beneficiary always has the option of taking more out of the account. Therefore, if you inherit an IRA, your immediate goal is to name a beneficiary so that they can take advantage of this rule if you die with a balance in the account.

IRA Spousal Rollovers

Our legal system, much like our tax code, makes special considerations for spouses. From filing a joint tax return to tax-free spousal gifts, spouses have special rights and opportunities as beneficiaries. The problem that arises with having multiple options as a spouse is the possibility of making a wrong choice that results in a costly consequence. When a spouse is a beneficiary, he or she can always choose to rollover. Non-spouse beneficiaries cannot rollover; they can only remain as beneficiaries. A spouse has more options than any other type of beneficiary regardless of when the IRA owner dies.

HORSE SENSE

Spousal beneficiaries can also stay as beneficiaries on an inherited account or rollover. Non-spouse beneficiaries receive an inherited account only.

Let's look at an example. John Smith leaves his IRA to his 46 year-old daughter, Sue. Sue can take RMDs from her inherited IRA over her life expectancy of 37.9 years. If Sue passes away at age 60, her beneficiary, Emma, can continue taking distributions over Sue's remaining schedule. Emma does not have the option of using her own life expectancy because she is not the original beneficiary. She is stuck with the schedule of the original beneficiary.

An Important Exception for Certain Spousal Inherited IRAs

There is an exception to being "stuck" with the **decedent's** (the person who passed away) life expectancy payout. Let's say that a spouse is the beneficiary, and rather than rolling over, she decides to remain the beneficiary on the inherited IRA. The spouse then names her daughter as the inherited IRAs beneficiary. If the surviving spouse dies prior to the date the account owner would have reached age 70½ (the required beginning date for distributions), the beneficiary's beneficiary (the daughter), gets to use her own life expectancy when computing the post-death required minimum distributions. When a surviving spouse remains as beneficiary of the IRA, and then dies prior to turning age 70½, the spouse is treated as the IRA owner. Therefore, the daughter is considered the designated beneficiary and gets to stretch over her own life expectancy. This is the only exception to the rule.

DON'T TRIP UP!

If you are under age 59½, and your spouse dies with an IRA, do not choose a rollover if you feel you may need money. Instead, remain as a beneficiary until the age of 59½. This will allow for penalty-free distributions from the inherited IRA until you, as the surviving spouse, reach age 59½. Then the surviving spouse can perform a rollover into an IRA. This transforms the individual from a beneficiary to the owner of a new IRA, allowing him or her to defer required distributions if they are under age 70½.

Non-spouse beneficiaries have no choice. They must remain as beneficiaries and, as mentioned earlier in the chapter, they can take money out penalty free because it is a death distribution.

There are two payments that beneficiaries need to worry about. If the deceased did not take an RMD in the year of death, the beneficiary must take it for them based on the deceased's distribution schedule. This money is paid to the beneficiary and is a taxable event for the beneficiary. Once that yearly payment is made, in the next full year, the distribution must be taken by the end of the next calendar year as the required minimum distribution for the beneficiary. The beneficiary of the inherited IRA must take any unpaid RMD in the year of the decedent's death. Then, the first distribution must be taken from an inherited IRA by December 31st in the year following the deceased IRA owner's year of death. An up-to-date RMD Worksheet (see Appendix A) will help you keep track of distributions, and help your tax preparer, spouse, and beneficiaries after you're gone. A good financial advisor will also have this information in your file.

Threats to the "Stretch" IRA

Not only do you have to make sure that you name your beneficiaries, but you have to make sure that your IRA custodian will allow for such things. This is where you want to do your homework to determine if your IRA custodian will allow your beneficiary to then name their beneficiary once you've passed away and your IRA is inherited. This is more important than people think.

We discussed it, but let's review an example. Your beneficiary has a life expectancy of 50 years, meaning he is allowed a fifty year timeframe to stretch your IRA. But imagine if the beneficiary dies with 30 years left on the schedule and assets in the account. It is imperative that the IRA custodian allow your beneficiary, when he inherits the IRA from you, to name a new beneficiary. This allows the last beneficiary to continue the remaining thirty year schedule of the stretch. If the custodian does not allow this, the inherited IRA will go through probate at the death of the original beneficiary and the tax advantages of the stretch are lost.

Ask about your IRA custodian's rules in the following circumstances:

- When no beneficiary is named on an IRA (who is the default beneficiary?)
- When the beneficiary cannot find the form
- When the IRA custodian cannot find the form (this happens a lot due to the number of mergers that are taking place in financial businesses)

DON'T TRIP UP!

If the custodian says that the default beneficiary is the estate, and you are a spouse—you need this information to plan ahead. IRAs do not pass through probate unless the beneficiary designation or default beneficiary is the estate. As a spouse you want to avoid this, since spouses have special treatment when named the beneficiary of an IRA. Perform a trustee-to-trustee transfer to a custodian whose default beneficiary is not the estate.

Does the IRA custodian allow your children or grandchildren to move the inherited IRA to a different custodian after you pass away? You do not want your beneficiaries to be essentially handcuffed to a poor custodian or an unfavorable merger. We are not talking about a spousal rollover, where the option of changing the custodian is always available. When the beneficiary is not your spouse, he or she is no longer eligible for a rollover. In this instance, the beneficiary can only perform trustee-to-trustee transfers. Because of this rule, make sure the benefits of your IRA are portable. Contrary to popular opinions, some custodians are much better than others. You want your survivors to have the ability to transfer the dollars to the custodian of their choice.

If you would like to fill out a power of attorney form, you must make sure that the custodian of your IRA will accept your form. Some will want their own power of attorney agreement on file. It's important that you understand your custodian's policy while you're healthy, competent, and can get together the necessary paperwork. If, prior to death, the IRA owner is incapacitated (or otherwise unable to make decisions) often a trusted family member or advisor, through the use of a power of attorney form, will have the ability to make required minimum distributions, make investment decisions, change beneficiaries, etc. Likewise, you want the option of allowing someone else to act on your behalf to save potential stretch options of your IRA. Therefore, if your custodian will not accept your power of attorney, simply request their specific power of attorney form, and fill it out completely and make sure your custodian has it on file.

How will inherited IRA benefits be distributed if one of the beneficiaries dies prior to the account owner? For example, let's say that you are one of four siblings. Your mother has named you all beneficiaries of her IRA. If your brother predeceases your mother, who will get his share of your mother's retirement account? Will it go to your brother's family (his wife and children), or will his share be divided up by the custodian and go to the surviving siblings? Assuming that you want to make sure that the deceased's sibling's family does not get disinherited, you want to inquire if the custodian will allow for what is called the **per stirpes provision** (meaning "by the blood,") which allows for the deceased siblings share to pass onto his or her family members. Otherwise, when a beneficiary dies, the IRA owner must change his beneficiary agreement to name the spouse and/or offspring of the deceased beneficiary. It's much easier and efficient to use a custodian which permits the per stirpes provision.

FROM THE HORSE'S MOUTH

You also want to ask if your IRA custodian allows your IRA to be split via the beneficiary agreement after you have died. This allows each beneficiary to stretch over their life expectancy and control their own destiny. If your beneficiaries cannot split the account, they must stretch over the oldest beneficiary's life expectancy. As we've discussed earlier, this is not the most advantageous method available to most beneficiaries. If your custodian won't let you split post-death, think about finding a new custodian. The sooner, the better!

Your beneficiaries must keep a close eye on the IRA custodian when performing a spousal rollover or when they chose to re-title the inherited IRA. If the custodian accidentally issues a check to the beneficiaries, it will become a taxable event—and the benefits of the stretch are lost. If the custodian transfers money from the inherited IRA into the beneficiary's IRA, it will be considered both an illegal contribution and a taxable event, voiding any possibility of a stretch. Any of these potential mishaps will cause immediate taxation. Be forewarned: this happens more often than you could possibly imagine. To be safe, find a financial advisor who has plenty of IRA experience, who will help you find a good custodian and steer you clear of problematic custodians.

IRA Beneficiary Information

This information is not a designated beneficiary form. This is for informational purposes only to provide your beneficiaries with information about your retirement accounts. Each retirement account should have its own information sheet. Be sure to update your actual beneficiary designation forms often.

Financial Institution _____

Financial Representative _____

Address _____

Phone Number _____

Account Number _____

Location of Beneficiary Designation Form _____

Primary Beneficiary/(s)

NAME	TAX I.D. #	SHARE OF BENEFITS
1.		
2.		
3.		

Contingent Beneficiary/(s)

NAME	TAX I.D. #	SHARE OF BENEFITS
1.		
2.		
3.		

NOTES

CHAPTER 5

CASHING OUT: MINIMUM DISTRIBUTION RULES

W hat goes up must come down. And what goes in an IRA must come out, eventually. The IRS rules on Required Minimum Distributions (RMDs) dictate *when* money must be taken out of retirement accounts. These rules were established by Congress in the Tax Reform Act of 1986. They have been through a number of revisions since. These rules state that retirement plan owners must take annual distributions from their accounts regardless of whether they need the money or not. Such forced distributions are referred to as required minimum distributions (RMDs)—which we've discussed in previous chapters. The sole exception to RMDs is the Roth IRA, which we'll cover in the next chapter.

Required minimum distributions are triggered when retirement plan owners reach age 70½. Since, as the name implies, they are *minimum* requirements, it's important to note that you can always take distributions at an earlier age. As a reminder though, if you take distributions before age 59½, most distributions will be subject to penalties. Once required minimum distributions have begun, they must continue for the duration of the account owner's lifetime. We are often asked why the IRS settled on age 70½. We don't have a clue! We have yet to meet someone who can explain it to us. If you figure it out, please let us know!

As a rule of thumb, if your birthday is between January and June, the year in which you turn age 70 is the first year that the IRS requires you take a minimum distribution. If your birthday falls in July through December, age 71 is your first required distribution year.

The date by which distributions are required to commence is called the required beginning date (RBD). Each year's RMD is due December 31st, with an exception available for the first distribution year. That distribution can be delayed until April 1st of the following year.

DON'T TRIP UP!

If the account owner fails to take his RMD, a penalty is assessed by the IRS. The penalty is a 50% tax on the difference between the amount that should have been distributed and what was actually distributed.

As an example, if your RMD was $1,000 and you only took $500, you'll receive a 50% penalty on the $500 shortfall ($250 penalty). If you take out more than your RMD, the amount you will have to take in future years won't be reduced. So, if your RMD was $1,000, and you actually took $2,000, you cannot use the $1,000 overage against future RMDs.

Until recently, if you failed to take your full RMD, chances were the IRS wouldn't find out. That is now changing. One of the main features of the new tax rules is that IRA custodians are required to notify both you and the IRS that you have an RMD. Since you will be notified, it will become more difficult to apply an ignorance defense—and meanwhile hope the IRS takes pity on you and waives the penalty. Starting in 2004, IRA custodians were required to notify the IRS which customers were due to take a RMD, although the IRS isn't be notified as to the exact dollar amount.

HORSE SENSE

It is usually best not to postpone your first year's required distribution unless your income tax bracket will be much lower in the second year than it is in the first. By postponing your first year's distribution, you are forced to take two distributions in the second year. You are also making more work for yourself, because you will have different deadlines for each distribution, in addition to two different account values to compute each year's distribution and two different divisors for your calculations. You increase the risk of making a mistake that can cost you money in the form of penalties and interest.

Why Do Minimum Distribution Rules Exist?

The government has patiently allowed you to accumulate money under the umbrella of tax deferral and now the government wants its fair share. The government established rules for retirement plans to make sure these accounts are used to supplement retirement income—not to build an estate for heirs. Distributions from retirement plans are included as gross income on your tax return, as a taxable event. Uncle Sam finally gets his piece of your pie. The rules impose no maximums on distributions; you are free to withdraw as much as you like at any time. The government would love everyone to empty their IRAs immediately—it would be more money in their pockets.

> ## HORSE SENSE
>
> *If you have multiple IRAs, try to take your RMD from the smallest IRA. The goal is to try and reduce the number of IRAs you own. This will make RMD planning easier and will greatly simplify estate planning for the beneficiaries of your IRAs.*

Computing the Distribution

RMDs are calculated annually by dividing the year-end account balance by your applicable divisor. The divisor is found in the uniform distribution table, except in two cases: a) designated beneficiaries (designated beneficiaries must always be individuals who are alive) and you can use the Single Life Table to compute RMDs from inherited retirement accounts; and b) in cases where a spouse is the sole beneficiary and more than ten years younger than the account owner you can use the Joint and Last Survivor Table. Your financial advisor has access to these tables, but you can also find them online on some IRA-related sites (such as www.irs.gov).

As of 2003, the Uniform Distribution Table divisor used to compute your RMD is figured as if your beneficiary were ten years younger than your age. This works to the advantage of anyone whose beneficiary is less than ten years younger, as the required distributions will be smaller than the distribution would have been under the old rules.

As mentioned earlier, if your spouse is the sole beneficiary and is more than ten years younger, you won't use the Uniform Lifetime Table. You both get the benefit of using of your actual joint life expectancy. Your applicable divisor will be found in the Joint and Last Survivor Table.

As far as computing lifetime RMDs, most taxpayers will find that their annual required distribution has been decreased under the

HORSE SENSE

Appendix A contains a worksheet that makes it easy to keep track of your RMDs. This information will be very helpful for your own organization, but also useful to your tax preparer and beneficiaries. Make sure you inform your beneficiaries of the location of your account information!

new legislation. This is good news, since you can always take more than the minimum.

To figure out your RMD, start with your combined IRA account balances as of December 31st of the prior year and divide the balance by your applicable divisor. For example, if your balance on 12/31/2004 was $512,000, and you will be 72 in 2005, your divisor will be 25.6. Your RMD is $512,000 divided by 25.6, or $20,000.

Remember to look at the actual type of retirement accounts you own and, more importantly, remember to take the proper distribution from each type. If you have four different IRAs spread across a bank, a mutual fund, a brokerage firm and a credit union, you must compute the aggregate RMD for all your IRAs. The actual distribution can be taken from any one IRA; you do not have to take pro rata distributions from each. The same holds true for multiple 403(b) accounts.

Let's take another look at an example. You own:

- A 401(k) held by your employer from a previous job
- An IRA at the bank
- A second IRA at the XYZ brokerage firm
- A third IRA at a mutual fund company
- You are also the beneficiary of an inherited IRA

DON'T TRIP UP!

• *You cannot take a distribution from an IRA to satisfy the RMD due from your 403(b), and vice versa.*

• *If you are the owner of an IRA and also a beneficiary of an inherited IRA, you cannot take a distribution from an IRA that you own to satisfy a RMD for the inherited IRA, and vice versa.*

• *Do not aggregate in any combination: inherited IRAs; owned IRAs or 403(b) retirement accounts. You cannot combine account values for different types of retirement plans when taking RMDs. We tell clients that you can only add up accounts—you can't mix different flavors!*

Based on the account balances and your divisor, you have calculated your RMDs to be: $1,000 for your 401(k), $2,000 from the IRA at the bank, $3,000 from the IRA at the XYZ brokerage firm, $4,000 from the IRA at the mutual fund company—for a total of $9,000 required from IRAs. You also have $5,000 from the inherited IRA. Since you cannot combine the 401(k) RMD with the RMD from your IRAs, you must take the $1,000 distribution directly from the 401(k). You do not have to take a distribution from each account but can take a distribution from one IRA or any combination of IRAs as long as the total distributed equals or exceeds the $9,000 required in this example. You also may not combine distributions from IRAs you own with IRAs you are the beneficiary of to satisfy your RMD. Instead, you must take the $5,000 distribution directly from the inherited IRA.

FROM THE HORSE'S MOUTH

If you had more than one inherited IRA from the same decedent, you can aggregate the inherited IRAs for RMD purposes—just as you have for the IRAs you own. Take the RMD from one or any combination of the inherited IRAs.

The latest changes in the RMD laws, which have resulted in significantly smaller amounts being forced out of IRAs in the form of RMDs, allow for more potential growth of the account over the owner's lifetime. Depending upon the rate of return in the account, there could actually be more in the account at the owner's death than when the owner started to take RMDs.

For example, if the account owner takes only the RMDs each year (beginning at his RBD), and earns an average of 6%, the account will have the same value when the owner is 89 than when he started distributions at 70½. This is simply because the overall distributions were more than made up by earnings.

HORSE SENSE

If your IRA is fully invested (with no cash is held in the account) the IRA lacks the cash to take your RMD, take the distribution in kind. This means that you take out the asset in the same form it was held in the IRA. When your taxes are due, usually April 15th of the following year, you will pay taxes due on the distribution.

To take an in kind distribution, instead of selling something in the IRA and taking the distribution in cash, you take the equivalent dollar amount of whatever the account holds. Tell your custodian that you would like to take your distribution in shares of your mutual funds, stocks, individual bonds, or any combination of what is held in the account.

The day the distribution is made, simply add up the market value of the distributed securities to get your exact distribution dollar amount. The value of those securities on the date distributed becomes your cost basis. As a rule of thumb, take distributions of securities you believe will appreciate over time but may be temporarily undervalued. The assets, if held more than one year, will qualify for long term capital gains rates. If they are held until you die, your heirs will receive a step up in basis.

Postponing RBD

If you are over 70½ and are still employed by a company that offers a qualified retirement plan, you may postpone the RMD until you retire if the plan allows this. If you have an IRA in addition to being a member of a qualified retirement plan, you may roll your IRA into the company's plan, if the custodian allows that kind of transfer. The IRA is now part of the plan and RMDs can be postponed until retirement.

In order to postpone RMDs, the employee cannot own more than 5% of the company. 5% includes ownership of outstanding shares or total combined voting power. If the employer is not a corporation, 5% ownership of capital or profits inclusive of stock options as well as holdings of related individuals and entities will disqualify the postponing of RBD.

As an example, Fred is age 75 and works for the XYZ Company. He is not a 5% owner, and he participates in XYZ's retirement plan. The plan allowed Fred to roll his IRA into the company's retirement plan as well as a retirement plan Fred had from a previous employer. The XYZ Company is the employer maintaining the plan which now holds Fred's IRA assets and his old retirement plan assets. Fred is not required to take RMDs until April 1st in the year following his retirement from XYZ. This date will become his new RBD.

DON'T TRIP UP!

Use caution when applying the rules for postponing RBDs to 403(b) plans because some are not plans at all! Instead, they are annuity contracts purchased by the employer for the employee. The employer does not, in fact, maintain the plan but only buys the annuity contract. In this case, the employee would not be allowed to postpone his RBD by continuing to work.

The IRS recently issued a Private Letter Ruling approving another method of delaying RMDs. The situation involved a taxpayer who was employed by two companies. He was a 5% owner in one company (Company A), but not in the other (Company B). The taxpayer participated in both companies' qualified retirement plans. When he reached age 70½ in 2004, his RBD became April 1, 2005 for the retirement account at the company where he was a 5% owner.

The taxpayer stated to the IRS that he intended to withdraw his 2004 RMD by December 31, 2004, and then wanted to roll over the remaining retirement account balance from Company A to the company he was not a 5% owner of, Company B. The ruling explains that both plans would allow an in-service withdrawal and would accept eligible rollover distributions. The ruling request asked for confirmation that he would not be required to receive a distribution from the plan he rolled over to until he reaches his RBD under the plan, which would be April 1 of the year after he retires. The IRS agreed and allowed for the postponement of RMDs.

Naming IRA Beneficiaries

Most people do not realize the importance of the IRA beneficiary designation form they filled out when they opened their account. Everyone knows where to find their will and trust documents. But few people hold the beneficiary agreement in the same high regard, even though it can be much more important to your surviving family than your will (which does not cover your IRA). As we said in Chapter 2, IRAs pass to beneficiaries outside of the will. They pass by contract, which means the money follows the beneficiary agreement, *no matter what your will says.* Many people are shocked to hear this. The beneficiary designation form is, in fact, the estate planning document for your IRA.

Too many investors do not know where to find their beneficiary designation forms. If you cannot find your form, request a new one from your custodian. These forms can be updated as often as you like. Once replaced with an updated form, you should be sure to keep it in a safe place and let your beneficiaries know where it is. Always plan for the worst and expect the IRA custodian to not have an updated copy.

DON'T TRIP UP!

It is a good idea to periodically ask for a copy of the beneficiary form that your custodian has on file to ensure it matches your most updated form. Reasons to update the form include: any life changing event, the birth of a grandchild, a marriage, a divorce, or a death in the family.

You cannot be too detailed when filling out the beneficiary form. If you have four children who will share equally, spell out clearly that each child will receive 25% of the IRA upon your death—so there is no potential confusion. As an example, an IRA owner hadn't updated his beneficiary form since he started his IRA in the 1980. When he opened the account, he only had one child. At that point, he named his firstborn as the beneficiary. Twenty-five years later, he has four children, and decides that he would like each to share equally after he goes. There's one big problem: the beneficiary form was never updated, so the custodian considers only the eldest child the sole beneficiary of the IRA. The oldest child was well aware of the parent's wish, so what does she do if her parents unexpectedly die before they update the paperwork? She should cash out the entire IRA, which had grown to $2 million, pay income tax on the entire balance (which added up to over $600,000), then disperse each sibling's share of the balance.

Two things happen in this scenario. First, the children lose the ability to stretch that $2 million over their lifetimes (the "stretch" concept is detailed in Chapter 3). This alone can cost the family millions of dollars. Second, the eldest child had to include $2 million as gross income. So, she alone had to pay the tax in one tax return, instead of spreading the tax burden over the four tax returns that would have been involved if the beneficiary form had been correctly filled out in this example.

This caused an increase in the overall taxes being paid on the $2,000,000, due to our progressive tax system. Think of it this way—spreading a dollar due in tax as 25 cents reported over four tax returns will cause less tax due than one person reporting the entire dollar as gross income. More money was immediately squandered in the form of one tax return footing the bill and the family lost out on a potential fortune with the lost stretch. All of this was due to lack of attention to the IRA beneficiary form—which wouldn't have taken twenty minutes of her father's time.

Don't Trip Up!

In addition to primary beneficiaries, don't forget to also include contingent beneficiaries in the event that a primary beneficiary dies before the account owner.

Designated Beneficiary

By definition, a beneficiary is a legal entity which is entitled to any remaining balance in an account, should the account owner die before the account is depleted. There can be multiple beneficiaries on an IRA and a beneficiary does not have to be a person. It can also be a charity, trust or estate.

However, *a designated beneficiary must be a person or trust that qualifies as a designated beneficiary.* So, what is a designated beneficiary? It is necessary to pay IRA balances over a life expectancy—to "stretch" the IRA. Not every beneficiary qualifies as a designated beneficiary, so not every beneficiary is allowed the benefits of the stretch provision. We've heard it said that a designated beneficiary must have two things to qualify: a) a birthday, and b) a pulse. But there is a third qualification—the person must have a Social Security number. Only people can be designated beneficiaries—what else has a birthday, a pulse, and a Social Security number? Moreover, why? To stretch RMDs, a beneficiary must have a measurable life expectancy according to IRS tables. And don't get funny about naming your favorite pet as a beneficiary. That's why the Social Security number is required. If this is an actual concern in your situation, set up a trust if you want an animal to benefit from your money when you're gone.

No Named Beneficiary

What if you never named a beneficiary or if the form can't be found? Each IRA custodian has a default provision when no beneficiary is listed. The most common default provision is to have the IRA owner's estate become the beneficiary. This is normally not a good choice. This will result in an accelerated payout of the IRA after the account owner's death, and could subject the account to probate. There are few, if any, benefits to naming your estate as beneficiary. Unfortunately, there are many disadvantages.

The ability to take advantage of the "stretch" concept is immediately lost when the estate is beneficiary. Remember, there must be a pulse and a birthday to stretch an IRA, and the estate has neither. Failing to name a beneficiary is the logical reason for an IRA custodian to revert to the default provision, but it may not be that simple. If your heirs cannot find the beneficiary designation form, or the IRA custodian cannot find it for some reason, your family is stuck with the default. This is not a good position for your heirs.

When Are Beneficiaries Recognized?

The beneficiaries listed on the day of the account owner's death are those who will receive the inherited IRA. But, for tax purposes and for determining the maximum time RMDs for beneficiaries can be stretched, the family has until September 30th *of the year following the year of the IRA owner's death* (the **designation date**) to determine the designated beneficiaries. This doesn't mean the family can add names to the beneficiary form after the IRA owner has died. Only the account owner can change the beneficiaries, and that can only be done while alive. The beneficiaries can only be changed when a designated beneficiary opts not to receive any benefits (called **disclaiming**). The disclaiming beneficiary's share of the benefits then flow—according to the beneficiary agreement—to the remaining beneficiaries.

When an IRA owner dies, the beneficiary's payout period for taking RMDs from the inherited IRA is based on life expectancy, or the maximum number of years over which IRA assets can be withdrawn.

Spousal Options

A spouse has the most flexibility when named as beneficiary. The IRS allows a surviving spouse the most liberal taxation options versus non-spousal beneficiaries. The most popular option when the IRA owner dies is for the spouse to rollover the deceased's IRA into her own IRA. It allows the spouse to transfer the IRA and the property then falls to the spouse.

The transfer can be accomplished in one of two ways:

- An actual rollover occurs when the spouse withdraws the balance and then re-deposits the money into her own IRA (within the sixty day grace period the IRS allows to avoid paying taxes on the rollover amount);
- The second option is a direct trustee-to-trustee transfer. With a direct transfer, the funds are moved directly from the deceased IRA owner's account into the spouse's IRA without the spouse ever physically touching the funds.

The direct transfer (or trustee-to-trustee transfer) is, by far, the most efficient method to rollover IRA funds. There are fewer moving parts, there is no check to lose, and there is no sixty day countdown to get the funds deposited into a spousal IRA. All these factors mean there is less risk of the transfer causing a taxable event.

Moreover, once the money is transferred or rolled over, the spouse is no longer a beneficiary of an inherited IRA, but, instead, the owner of the IRA. The IRS deems the spouse to have always been the owner of the IRA, and RMDs will be determined by the spouse's age and life expectancy. If the spouse is under 70½, she can postpone RMDs until she reached her RBD *even if her late spouse was already taking RMDs.* If the spouse is over 70½, when the account is inherited, the spouse must begin taking RMDs by December 31st of the year following the IRA owner's death.

Death Prior to RBD

What happens when an IRA owner dies prior to his RBD? Non-spousal beneficiaries have two methods for taking distributions (distributions are mandatory for non-spouse beneficiaries) from an inherited IRA or qualified plan. The first is the five-year rule which generally requires all money to be distributed to the beneficiaries before the end of the fifth calendar year after the year the account owner dies. In this scenario, if the account owner died in 2010, all money must be removed from the inherited account by December 31st, 2015. However, an exception to the five-year rule allows your IRA to take advantage of the "stretch" option, but your plan must elect to do so otherwise the five-year rule goes into effect automatically.

The second method of determining payout schedules from inherited retirement accounts is the **life expectancy method**. This is what we have been harping on for the last fifty pages or so. This allows the beneficiary a long and profitable tax deferred distribution schedule. We are always making one very large assumption with deferred payout schedules—that the beneficiary can overcome the "need" for a new Mercedes in the driveway.

There is no distribution necessary in year of death because the account owner passed before the RBD. Distributions must begin by December 31st of the year following the year of death or the IRS will disallow the extended payout schedule (life expectancy method) and force the five year rule.

Spousal Choices

Let's say that John is an IRA owner who passed away in 2004, at age 66. His 62 year-old wife, Martha, is sole beneficiary. She rolls John's IRA into her own IRA, with no RMD necessary. She is now the account owner, but since she has not reached her RBD, so she can postpone RMDs until she turns 70½ in 2012. In this scenario, she has delayed RMDs an additional four years, compared to when John would have been forced to start RMDs in 2008.

Let's look at the same situation, but make his wife Martha age 72 when John dies. She completes an IRA transfer, just as she did in the prior example. Even though she is past her RBD, she does not have to take a RMD in 2004, because John died before his RBD. Starting in 2005, Martha will have to begin taking RMDs because she is past her RBD, and her husband's IRA is now her property. Martha will look to the Uniform Lifetime Table for her life expectancy (her divisor) and divide that into her aggregate IRA balances as of December 31, 2004 to determine her RMD.

Death Post-RBD

How are things different when an IRA owner dies after his Required Beginning Date, and has already begun taking (or is obligated to take) a RMD? If his money is in a qualified plan, he must first check the plan's rules. If money is in an IRA, the remaining balance must be distributed at least as rapidly as under the distribution schedule being used in the year of death. In the years following the account owner's death, there are two schedules.

If there is a designated beneficiary, the distribution period is the LONGER of:

- the remaining life expectancy of the deceased
- the life expectancy of the designated beneficiary

If no designated beneficiary exists, the distribution period is the remaining life expectancy of the deceased account owner.

DON'T TRIP UP!

By now all non-spouse beneficiaries know they must take a RMD for the deceased in the year of death using the schedule that was in existence. But what about next year? The beneficiary will not use the Uniform Lifetime Table, but must use the Single Life Expectancy Table going forward (see Appendix A). Failure to switch to the correct table will result in RMDs that are much smaller than is required by the IRS and then they'll want their excise tax!

Spousal Options

Let's say John dies at age 76 leaving his 62 year-old wife, Martha, as beneficiary. When Martha rolls John's IRA into her own, she doesn't have to begin RMDs until she reaches 70½, her RBD. If

John did not take his RMD in 2004 (prior to his death), Martha must take his RMD before she begins rolling the IRA over into her own name. She cannot roll, and then take the RMD, because the property will already be hers. Failure to take John's RMD in his year of death would cause a 50% penalty on any amount that should have been withdrawn but was not. The RMD Martha takes for John in 2004 cannot be rolled over.

Let's again take the same situation but make the wife 10 years older. John dies at age 76 in 2004, but now Martha is age 72. John did not take his RMD for 2004 prior to his death so Martha must take John's RMD *for him*, prior to rolling his IRA over. Since Martha is past her RBD, she must take her RMD in 2005. She will use the Uniform Lifetime Table to find her life expectancy factor to divide into her 12/31/2004 balance.

DON'T TRIP UP!

Once the rollover occurs, it becomes the spouse's property—so make sure to clearly list the spouse's Social Security number on her IRA.

When Should a Spouse NOT Roll Over or Transfer?

A surviving spouse does not have to rollover the IRA. In fact, in some cases it makes sense not to perform the rollover at all. There are two fairly common situations where spousal rollovers aren't the sensible option:

1. If the surviving spouse is under 59½, and needs access to the IRA for living expenses, she shouldn't rollover. By rolling over the IRA, the IRS would assess the widow a 10% premature withdrawal penalty because she is under age 59½.

By remaining as a beneficiary, the spouse will avoid any early withdrawal penalties, because the distributions from an inherited IRA are considered death distributions and are not subject to the penalty regardless of the age of the beneficiary. When the surviving spouse turns 59½, she can then roll the inherited IRA into her own IRA. With this move, the IRA will become her property, and she'll therefore no longer be subject to the early withdrawal penalty. More importantly, she will use her own age to determine when she must begin her RMDs. (Note: if the widow knows she won't need any of the money to live on, she can rollover or transfer into her own IRA right away to avoid RMDs until her age 70½.)

2. If the surviving spouse is much older than the deceased IRA owner, she has the option to use the deceased spouse's life expectancy to compute RMDs (rather than her own life expectancy). Using the deceased's longer life expectancy will produce smaller RMDs than those required if the beneficiary rolled the IRA over and used her own life expectancy. The news gets better if the surviving spouse was older than the deceased IRA owner, and the IRA owner passed away prior to his RBD. By remaining a beneficiary, the older spouse does not have to begin taking RMDs until the year the deceased younger spouse would have turned 70½.

Once the spousal beneficiary reaches her RBD, it is generally preferable for her to roll the remaining inherited IRA balance over. Why? Because the spouse is then able to use the **Uniform Lifetime Table** to her benefit. The Uniform Lifetime Table calculates the divisor as if the beneficiary is ten years younger than she actually is to determine her RMD. This is much more favorable than being forced to use the Single Life Expectancy Table that beneficiaries must use to calculate RMDs. Using the Uniform Lifetime Table will result in smaller RMDs than using the Single Life Table. Smaller RMDs equal a smaller tax bill, and more money to continue the stretch. For a diagram of this principle, see Appendix A.

HORSE SENSE

Making a decision about performing a spousal rollover or remaining a beneficiary is not an all or nothing proposition. A portion of the investment can be rolled over with the remaining balance left in the inherited IRA for the beneficiary to access if necessary. As a beneficiary, there are still RMD regulations that must be taken by December 31st of the year the IRA owner would have turned 70½, or December 31st of the year following the IRA owner's death, whichever comes later.

More Spousal Benefits of Inherited IRAs

We have just mentioned that a beneficiary must use the Single Life Table when computing RMDs. Spouses get advantages that non-spouse beneficiaries do not. Each year, a spousal beneficiary gets to recalculate her RMD divisor in the Single Life Table. Each year, she goes back to the table and uses the life expectancy for her age in the distribution year—recalculating. This is an advantage because your life expectancy increases incrementally each year, allowing you to stretch out the RMDs over a longer period of time, to an ever-older age!

There are two types of people who get to recalculate RMDs each year:

1. All IRA owners
2. Spousal beneficiaries

A non-spouse beneficiary must use a set term method. The non-spouse beneficiary looks up his or her life expectancy only once, in the first year a distribution is required. That factor is then reduced by one every year until the beneficiary dies or the account is emptied. Because a spouse who is recalculating each year has her life expectancy reduced by less than one year each year, according to the table, the spouse's RMDs are less than a non-spouse beneficiary's RMDs, even if they both began taking RMDs at the same age.

Let's look at the effect of recalculating versus non-recalculating. A spouse, who is age 49 in 2004, inherits an IRA from her 72 year-old husband. Rather than perform a rollover, she remains a beneficiary. The year after her husband dies, she will be 50 (2005), so she looks up the life expectancy of a 50 year-old from the Single Life Table to get her divisor of 34.2. According to the table, her remaining life expectancy is 34.2 years. In 2006, when she will be 51, so she looks up her life expectancy and it is 33.3. Even though she is one year older, her life expectancy factor has only decreased by 0.9. A non-spouse beneficiary's life expectancy is reduced by 1.0. Over time this difference can add up to significant savings in reduced RMDs. She will continue this process every year. Forty years from now, when she is 91 (in the year 2046), she will go back to the Single Life Table and look up the life expectancy of a 91 year-old (5.2 years).

Let's look at a non-spousal beneficiary in the same example. A 50 year-old child inherits his deceased mother's IRA. (Remember: non-spouse beneficiaries cannot roll over inherited IRAs, and can only remain a beneficiary.) The child will go to the same Single Life Table and look up his divisor as a fifty year-old. He finds that his divisor is 34.2 years, exactly like the previous example. That is the last time the divisor will be the same even though both examples began RMDs at age 50. The non-spouse cannot recalculate, so his divisor is reduced by one, and it continues to be reduced by one each and every year thereafter. The non-spouse is forced to empty the account by age 84.2. The spousal beneficiary, since she recalculates each year, can continue to stretch well past age 100!

Spousal Beneficiary Death

When the spousal beneficiary dies, what happens? Let's say John, the IRA owner, dies in 2004, at age 57, with his younger wife Martha as beneficiary. She is under 59½ at the time of John's death. Martha happens to get some good advice, so she decides to remain

DON'T TRIP UP!

Regardless of whether a spouse or non-spouse beneficiary inherits an IRA, new primary and contingent beneficiaries should be named immediately. Not naming new beneficiaries is the biggest mistake made in the transfer process for inherited and rolled over IRAs.

a beneficiary of the inherited IRA. This allows her penalty-free access to the IRA until she reaches 59½.

Martha immediately names her son Bill as beneficiary of her inherited IRA. Martha dies prior to her RBD. It just so happens that her husband, if he were still alive, would not yet have reached his RBD. Since Martha, his spousal IRA beneficiary, also died prior to her RBD, there is a special rule. By now you are probably sick to your stomach with rules, but press on!

In this special case, their son is allowed to use his own life expectancy to continue the stretch of his father's IRA, because the original account owner (John) died prior to what would have been his RBD, named his spouse (Martha) as beneficiary, and she was smart enough to name a beneficiary before she died. Bill will now calculate his RMDs using the Single Life Table and will recalculate each year as if he were a spousal beneficiary. Bill gets to stretch over his entire expected lifetime.

What if his mother forgot to name a beneficiary in this scenario? Bill can still inherit the IRA through Martha's estate but he must deplete the entire account over a five year time frame because of the five year rule. Martha is considered to be the IRA owner, and she died without a designated beneficiary. Her son Bill lost decades of stretch potential because his mother didn't name a beneficiary.

How does it change things when a spousal beneficiary dies after the original IRA owner would have reached RBD? When a spouse remains as beneficiary of an inherited IRA, and dies after the original IRA owner would have passed his RBD, a spousal beneficiary will benefit from an IRA paid out over her remaining life expectancy (based on her age in the year of her death). The Single Life Table is used, and the divisor is reduced each year by one, to calculate the beneficiary's RMD due from the inherited IRA.

Slightly modifying the above example, the original IRA owner dies at 64, when his spouse is 55. She decides to remain a beneficiary, and she dies 7 years later, at age 62. Since the IRA owner would have been past his RBD when his beneficiary died (age 64 + 7 yrs. = 71), the five year rule does not apply. We will take his wife's remaining life expectancy at the age that she died and go to the Single Life Table to get the applicable divisor for her RMDs. Each year that divisor is reduced by one to determine the RMD. The stretch is then limited to the spouse's remaining life expectancy, because she remained a beneficiary, and she died after the original IRA owner would have reached his RBD.

This is a potential disadvantage of the spouse remaining as a beneficiary rather than rolling the inherited IRA over. In this case, if the spouse had rolled the inherited IRA over and then named her son as beneficiary, Bill would be able to use his own life expectancy to stretch the remaining IRA balance. Bill would have been better served if his mother had performed a rollover or transfer, rather than remaining a beneficiary.

If the spouse had rolled or transferred and failed to name a designated beneficiary, the payout method would be determined by whether she died before or after her RBD. If she died prior to her RBD with no designated beneficiary, her heirs would be stuck with the five year rule. If she died on or after her RBD with no designated beneficiary, the account would be paid out over her remaining life expectancy in the year of her death from the Single Life Table.

In short: Name a designated beneficiary! This will not force the beneficiary to stretch the IRA but options are good.

HORSE SENSE

When a spouse dies prior to RBD, determine the optimal strategy by taking the following into account:

• *The number of years before the IRA owner would have hit RBD*

• *The number of years before the surviving spouse will reach his or her RBD*

• *The short-term and long-term income needs of the surviving spouse*

• *The health of the surviving spouse*

When an IRA owner names a non-spousal beneficiary, it doesn't matter if the original account owner dies before or after his RBD. Non-spousal designated beneficiaries use their own life expectancies from the Single Life Table to determine RMDs and the potential stretch period for an inherited IRA. The first distribution must be taken by December 31st of the year following the original account owner's year of death.

When the original IRA owner dies after his RBD, the designated beneficiary can stretch the inherited account over her own life expectancy using the Single Life Table exactly the same as a beneficiary who inherits an IRA from the account owner who died prior to his RBD. The only difference is that the beneficiary becomes responsible for taking the deceased's RMD in the year of death if the owner had not yet taken it.

The beneficiary must take the original account owner's RMD by December 31st in the year the owner died. The beneficiary will receive the distribution so the beneficiary is responsible for the taxes due because the RMD will be included in the beneficiary's gross income. The distribution does not get paid to the estate.

DON'T TRIP UP!

If the designated beneficiary is older than the original account owner, the beneficiary can use the deceased's life expectancy to calculate the post death RMDs. It is rare that the IRS will allow a beneficiary to stretch an IRA over a period of time that exceeds the beneficiary's life expectancy, but in this case it is allowed.

If the IRA owner dies after his RBD with no designated beneficiary, the IRA can be paid out over the deceased's life expectancy. Each future distribution will reduce the deceased's divisor by one to calculate the RMD. The five year distribution rule is only applicable to an IRA owner who dies prior to his RBD, if he didn't name a designated beneficiary. Remember: the birth date, pulse and Social Security rule still applies!

Estate as Beneficiary

It is usually not a good idea to name your estate as beneficiary because there will be no designated beneficiary, and, therefore, no opportunity for your family to take advantage of the stretch concept. An estate has no life expectancy, not to mention no pulse or birthday—all of which are required in a designated beneficiary. If the IRA owner died prior to reaching his RBD with his estate as beneficiary, the IRA has to be distributed over a five year period. If the owner died after his RBD, the IRA can be distributed over his remaining life expectancy. The estate is also subject to the highest income tax bracket (currently 35%) rather than the lower rates that apply to individuals.

When a retirement account passes through an estate, it is treated like any other probate asset, in that it is subject to the costs associated with probate and the benefits could be delayed in reaching your heirs. You lose the stretch and subject the IRA to costs and delays that could be associated with your estate. Wills are easily contested, leaving open the possibility that IRA money could be tied up in a lengthy, expensive lawsuit.

What if no beneficiary is named, but the surviving spouse is the sole beneficiary and executor of the estate? She has the opportunity to distribute the retirement benefits out of the plan to herself, and roll them over to her own IRA tax-free, as long as she completes the rollover within the sixty-day limit. This has been done many times through Private Letter Rulings (see Private Letter Ruling #2001-29036). A spouse must have the right to distribute the benefits to herself. If a third party has the right to distribute the benefits instead of the spouse, this strategy will not work.

What if the beneficiary form was not filled out in the smartest way? In extreme cases, you could try to have the naming of a beneficiary invalidated, in order to reinstate a more efficient beneficiary designation. To attempt this, the IRA owner would have to be found incompetent when he filled out his beneficiary designation form. This is a rare situation, and not one you'll want to count on.

For every rule there's an exception, and this is especially true when you're trying to translate and decipher IRS tax code. Here is another exception to the rule of thumb against naming your estate as beneficiary: If a substantial part of an individual's estate is in an IRA and the estate is going to be subject to estate tax, a portion of the IRA can be separated and the estate is named as beneficiary on that IRA. When the IRA owner dies, the estate taxes are paid from distributions from this IRA. When distributions are taken for the estate tax bill, there will also be income tax due from each dollar distributed from the IRA. This will allow the estate to receive the Income in Respect of a Decedent (IRD) deduction, which will reduce the overall income tax rate.

FROM THE HORSE'S MOUTH

Very high income individuals gradually lost the ability to take the deductions available to middle class tax-payers. Estates file income tax returns each year, but they don't lose the same deductions, no matter the amount of their income. This can make an estate look more at-tractive for post-death IRA distributions. Depending on the income of the people who you want to inherit your IRA, from an income tax planning point of view, they may be better off if you name a trust as the IRA beneficiary (instead of individuals). But, remember, when a trust is used, the individual beneficiaries may lose the stretch potential on the trust's portion. If there are no other funds available to pay the estate taxes then there wouldn't be any funds left to stretch anyway. Whew, that's heavy stuff. We may all need a break after that!

Charity as Beneficiary

The current tax laws are very favorable to people leaving a retirement account to charity or **charitable remainder trust** (CRT). A CRT is a trust that provides a **remainder** to one or more qualified charities. In other words, money left in the trust is eventually given to a charitable organization, such as a church, school, museum, or other social advocacy cause of your choice. The remainder is that portion of the trust which will eventually pass to a qualified charity.

Think of it this way: money that comes out of an IRA or quali-fied plan is subject to income tax, right? If you are charitably inclined, why not give away an asset that is eventually going to be taxed rather than an asset that will receive a step-up in basis for your heirs? If you have charitable intentions, consider using your IRA as a potential asset to be left to charity.

When planning to donate your IRA, the key is to separate whatever dollar amount you would like to leave to charity or CRT, and put it in a separate IRA to be used only for this purpose. This is the safest way to ensure your designated beneficiaries will be allowed the option to stretch the IRA. As an alternative to a separate IRA, you may also list the charity or CRT on the beneficiary form, clearly stating what percentage of the IRA will go to charity. As financial advisors, our personal preference is to use a completely separate account, which is a more organized, efficient way to handle your finances.

Let's take a look at an example of a particularly charitably-minded IRA owner. His IRA value is $50,000, and the owner names his child as beneficiary. It is also stated in the IRA owner's will that he has a charitable intent of $50,000 (of cash under his mattress) to his church. Under the current IRS rules, if the IRA owner changes the beneficiary designation to his church, there will be no changes to the owner's RMDs. Our IRA owner makes the church the beneficiary of his IRA, and changes his will, leaving the $50,000 (in cash) he would have given to the church, to his daughter instead. By doing so, his daughter gets $50,000 in cash from the estate rather than a $50,000 IRA that would be taxed over time.

When your situation involves a large IRA, and a large charitable intent, we advise you to examine your charitable giving options using software programs that are available today (at your financial advisor's or at many charities) to determine which scenario is most advantageous to you, your other beneficiaries and the charity.

The remainder in a CRT is irrevocable, meaning that once the trust is funded, there is no going back. In other words, the charitable beneficiary must receive the remainder at the end of the trust term. There may be a degree of flexibility in terms of naming and changing the charitable beneficiaries, and the trust may be drafted to allow the grantor or income beneficiaries to change the designated charitable beneficiaries. The trust's operation is defined and controlled by a number of federal statutes and regulations. If the trust qualifies under the statutes and regulations, there are significant income and transfer tax advantages.

> ## HORSE SENSE
>
> *The use of a CRT can be a valuable technique to control the ultimate disposition of wealth while reducing the client's income and transfer tax burden. The trust may be used as a source of income for the client or for other persons designated by the client, and is primarily used by those who have substantial wealth in addition to those assets that are placed into the trust.*

When the grantor contributes assets to a CRT, the grantor should get an immediate federal income tax deduction for the present value of the remainder. As we said earlier, the remainder is that portion of the trust which will eventually pass to a qualified charity. The amount of the deduction varies with the nature and value of the assets contributed to the trust, and the identity of the charitable beneficiary. The maximum deduction is received as a gift of cash to a public charity. Gifts of appreciated assets or gifts to private charities receive a lesser deduction.

The grantor is limited to taking the CRT deduction as a percentage of adjusted gross income. That portion of the income tax deduction that is not used in one year may be carried over for up to five years.

A properly operated CRT does not have to pay income tax on its transactions because it is a qualified charitable trust. When a highly-appreciated asset is used to fund a CRT, the trustee's sale of that asset and the recognition of capital gains is not a taxable event. This is a big deal! Instead, income tax is payable only when and to the extent the gain realized on the sale is distributed to the income beneficiary. These rules essentially mean that there is no cost to diversifying the portfolio if the trustee decides to sell assets. Further, the fact that the trust operates unburdened by income taxes allows for potentially better performance. The grantor (or the estate) will typically receive an estate or gift tax deduction for the value of the amount transferred to charity. The grantor has, in effect, named the charity as the beneficiary and cut the government out of receiving taxes on either the sale of the asset or when estate taxes are due.

The term of a CRT is set at twenty years, or for the remainder of a life of the grantor. When the trust is created, the grantor designates the method for determining the trust term. During the term of the trust, distributions are made to the income beneficiaries, in accordance with the provisions of the trust. While the grantor is normally one of the income beneficiaries, any individual may be named as the income beneficiary

DON'T TRIP UP!

What if you want to give money to charity, but you don't want to reduce the amount of money that goes to your family or other beneficiaries? Can you have your cake and donate it to a charity, too? Here's what many people do: They replace the wealth they have placed in the trust through the implementation of an Irrevocable Life Insurance Trust (ILIT), which we'll discuss later in the book. If you are charitably-minded, you'll want to work with an IRA advisor (AND an attorney) experienced with the creation and operation of CRTs, and the tax aspects of using this technique to fashion a complete lifetime game plan.

There are rigid requirements for CRTs and they are beyond the scope of this book, but you should know some of the nuances associated with CRTs. The annual payout methods come in two varieties to the non charitable beneficiaries, and will be clearly written in the trust document:

- One choice is for the trust to pay out a fixed dollar amount annually. The trust is called a Charitable Remainder Annuity Trust (CRAT).
- The second choice is for the trust to pay out a fixed percentage of the trust's value annually. In this case the CRT is called a Charitable Remainder Unit Trust (CRUT).

We won't discuss the details between the two in this book. However, we wanted to familiarize you with some phrases you might see in a CRT-specific book, and make sure you understood the mechanics of a CRT.

The CRT itself does not pay any income tax because it is tax exempt. Within the CRT, there is a very unique internal accounting system, called a four tier system. Every dollar that the CRT receives is allocated to one of the four tiers, based on the federal income tax character of the asset. There is ordinary income, capital gain, tax-exempt income or principal. The CRT recognizes the various types of income received into the trust. The CRT then assigns that type of tax treatment to the beneficiary when a distribution is made.

Too many people think that if they leave their IRA assets to the CRT, then the CRT takes a tax-free distribution. We've heard from clients who believe that, as a trustee, they can reinvest in tax-free municipal bonds, and then pay the tax-free interest to the non-charitable beneficiaries. Unfortunately, this isn't true, and doesn't work! The retirement plan distribution first has to fulfill the ordinary income tax tier, then the capital gains tax tier, then the tax-exempt income tier. So, even if the trust did invest the proceeds in tax-free bonds, distributions to those non-charitable beneficiaries would not be treated as tax exempt until all of the first tier (ordinary income tax) had been used up, and the second tier (capital gains tax) had been used up.

Therefore, although the CRT does not pay an income tax on its distribution from the retirement plan, the income beneficiary of the CRT will have to pay income tax on the CRT payments when received. The advantage of this is that when an IRA is left to a CRT, the estate is entitled to an estate tax deduction, according to an actuarially determined value of the remainder using IRS actuarial tables.

Here are two popular uses for the CRT as an IRA beneficiary:

1. If your retirement plan does not offer beneficiaries the ability to stretch the IRA—if it is in a qualified plan, for example—you might consider your CRT options. In circumstances where the IRA is going to your children, and the retirement plan does not allow the "stretch" for non-spouses, by naming the CRT beneficiary of the qualified plan, you will receive the estate tax benefits. This option may actually result in a longer, "stretch-like" payout provision for your children.

2. Leaving retirement assets to a CRT for a spouse's benefit has merit as well. The spouse will receive an income stream without the need for the spouse to perform a rollover of the IRA. The spouse can choose who the charitable beneficiary will be, and, if the spouse is the sole non-charitable beneficiary, there will be no estate tax due on the IRA money in the event of the IRA owner's death or the death of the surviving spouse. This is because of charitable and marital deductions. Without a CRT, if the spouse remains unmarried and dies with the money in her IRA, there could be estate taxes due.

DON'T TRIP UP!

There is nothing a trust can do to help eliminate taxes that cannot be done without a trust.

Trust as Beneficiary

When charities aren't being considered as an option, many people turn to a debate over the possibilities of IRAs left to trusts. Should you name a trust as an IRA beneficiary? The prevailing myth is that, by doing so, you will save taxes. Unfortunately, that's simply not true—it really is just a myth.

In fact, the only reason you would name a trust as your IRA beneficiary is to control or restrict access to the IRA principal after your death. Control or restriction might be important to you if the beneficiaries are minors, disabled, incompetent or unsophisticated, and you fear they might be taken advantage of, or if you want to ensure that the trustee will perform the stretch for the beneficiaries.

Often, it is difficult to decide your ultimate estate planning goals with so many options. For each scenario, there are both benefits and drawbacks. Additionally, with regard to using trusts, there are a couple of potential problems or, at the very least, disadvantages.

As an example of one right out of the starting gate: If money accumulates in a trust once it is distributed from the IRA, you could be subject to trust tax rates, which are much higher than individual tax rates. In 2010, if a trust accumulated or retained more than $11,200 of income, the trust tax rate reached 35%. Individuals do not reach the 35% threshold until they have taxable income over $326,500. So, you can see that trust income tax rates can be much higher than individual.

Let's assume you want to set up a trust. In this example, presuming that a trust is actually needed and worthwhile. You want to make sure that you do not fund the trust with IRA monies while you are alive, because once you do, you have taken a distribution, and you have to pay taxes and maybe penalties on that money. If the assets are placed in the trust, then they can no longer be in the IRA.

IRA rules clearly state that, to get the stretch, any designated beneficiary must have a birthday and a pulse, but there is one exception. When the IRS deems a trust to be what is called a "look-through" or "see-through" trust, it can be used for a stretch. The IRS will look under the hood of the trust to see if the designated beneficiaries can utilize the stretch concept.

The IRS has spelled out four requirements that the trust must have for the IRS to grant them "look-through" or "see-through" capabilities and status. If the trust qualifies, its beneficiaries will be considered as if they were named directly in the IRA. The four considerations that must be met include that:

1. The trust be valid under state law
2. The trust be irrevocable after death
3. Beneficiaries of the trust must be identifiable (they must be named)
4. A copy of the trust document must be delivered to the IRA custodian by October 31st in the year following the year of the IRA owners' death

DON'T TRIP UP!

The last requirement, to deliver a copy of the "look-through" or "see-through" trust to the IRA custodian by the stated deadline, is often overlooked. Forgetting to do this can negate the whole "look-through" treatment. Mark your calendar while you're planning!

Once the above requirements have been met, there are two types of trust that qualify for "look-through" or "see-through" status:

- A **conduit trust** exists where the IRA pays out RMDs (or more, if necessary) to the trust, and the trust immediately pays that money out to the beneficiary or beneficiaries. This is the most often used "look-through" or "see-through" trust. The distributions are then taxed to the beneficiaries at their personal rates. *Based on the life expectancy of the oldest trust beneficiary*, the applicable divisor is used to calculate the required minimum distributions. Since all income is paid out, there is no accumulation, and no trust tax rate problem.

- Unlike the conduit trust, a **discretionary** or **accumulation trust** may not pay all of the distributions received by the trust to the beneficiaries. It gives discretion to the trustee on whether all or part of the distribution received gets paid out. Any money that does not get paid out and remains in the trust gets taxed at trust rates. Within this trust, it must be very clear who the beneficiaries are, because the age of the oldest beneficiary is used for the required minimum distribution calculations.

With a discretionary trust, the IRS will look to determine who each beneficiary is and then use the life expectancy of the oldest beneficiary, who is usually a spouse, and therefore much older than the children. With this situation, you'll reduce your ability to "stretch." One thing that can remedy this is to separate the IRAs, and have a trust for each beneficiary. That way you get to use each beneficiary's own life expectancy for the trust.

As with all possibilities, there are some rules associated with trusts. With most trusts, it is very common to see the phrase "income being paid out," or "to pay for estate expenses." The reason you do not want to use these words is because the IRS might deem the estate your beneficiary. This is bad because it immediately kills the "stretch," as estates cannot be named designated beneficiaries. Because of this rule, use a specific trust to inherit the IRA, and a separate trust for the word "income" and for estate and expenses. All of this relates to the fact that IRAs have distribution rules while most other assets do not.

The reason you should not use the word "income" is because the IRS has actually already defined what can be considered income depending on the state you live in. The IRS definition of income, which could between 3-5% of the principal, might be different than the required minimum distributions. When you have a simple CD, and you note that the beneficiary should receive income for life, there is no problem. The principal remains in the trust and income is paid out. IRAs have RMD rules that force money out of the account at what could be a very different rate than the interest that is being paid on that principal. If the beneficiary lives long enough, all the money will eventually come out. Consequently, using the word "income" could result in a different amount than the RMD. Only use the word "income" in trusts that do not hold IRAs.

Problems with investments, specifically with IRAs, can often occur in second marriage situations. For instance, usually the IRA owner intends for his second wife to get income for the rest of her life, with the kids receiving the remaining balance. What actually happens, however, is that the kids become accidentally disinherited.

Here's how: If the IRA beneficiary is the trust, and the second wife lives long enough, the trust could actually be depleted and leave nothing left for the children. That might not be what the original IRA owner intended, but because of the trust wording, the second spouse will be entitled to much more than was originally planned. What you can do to avoid this scenario is to split the IRA into one IRA for the spouse and another for the kids. The spouse now has her own assets to live on, the kids are guaranteed to get their share, and they don't have to wait for the second spouse to pass away before they start receiving benefits.

Though frequently overlooked, there are some key points you must keep in mind if you want to make a trust the beneficiary of your IRA:

- Remember to list the trust as a beneficiary on the beneficiary designation form! All the work and cost of developing a trust can go to waste if it is not clearly stated that the trust is a beneficiary. Sounds simple enough, but many folks neglect this step.

- With an IRA, make sure that the custodian who holds the IRA will accept a trust as a beneficiary.

- If the money is in a qualified plan (a 401(k), for instance), you need to make sure that the plan document allows for a trust to be named as beneficiary. Often, it will not. Make sure to read the fine print and consult with your financial advisor.

- If you want your IRA to stretch, it becomes your responsibility to make sure that the trust qualifies as a "look-through" or "see-through" trust. Likewise, if you're hoping to utilize the stretch principle, make sure the estate is never listed or named by default in your planning. Estates considered as trust beneficiaries kill stretch potential.

Here are some other quick tips to keep in mind when contemplating the use of trusts.

- Make sure it is designated "beneficiaries only," not a charity (which is not a designated beneficiary).
- Don't use the word "income" in IRA trusts.
- Specifically name which IRA accounts you intend to be placed in the trust.
- The most important factor here is to make sure your beneficiaries do not have any surprises.
- To that end, make sure you clearly state to your trustee what exact payout methods you want.
- Tell the trustee ahead of time about your wishes.
- If you are considering a discretionary trust, the most efficient manner to fund it (and to avoid any potential tax rate problems) is to use a Roth IRA—it removes the entire taxable distribution problem.
- All trusts follow distribution rules for naming a non-spouse as a beneficiary, even if a beneficiary in the IRA trust is a spouse as sole beneficiary.
- Make sure, just like with any IRA beneficiary, that when naming a trust, you do so when the IRA owner is still alive.
- Very important! Remember that you do not fund the trust with the IRA; IRA money stays in the IRA. The only money that comes out of the IRA and goes into the trust is the

distribution and never the principal. As soon as the money comes out of the IRA, it becomes a taxable event.

- SEPs and SIMPLEs are still IRAs and follow the same rules as any other IRA.

- Keoghs are like 401(k)s. Depending on your plan documents, Keoghs might not allow a trust as a beneficiary, and they might force a lump sum payout at the owner's death.

- If you go through all the work of determining if you need a trust, make sure that you have it set up correctly. After the IRA owner passes away, it will be too late to any fix problems.

When you are buried in the process of determining if a trust is right for your family, consider that trusts exist purely for control, to restrict assets to the IRA principal after the IRA owner's death. They do nothing to save the family from taxes. Most significantly, you have to make sure the trust is set up correctly so that it will qualify for the much-needed "look-through" or "see-through" IRS approval. Lastly, once the IRA owner passes away, you want to be sure the beneficiaries implement the trust properly.

NOTES

CHAPTER 6

A SUPERFECTA: THE ROTH IRA

Introduced in 1998, through the Taxpayer Relief Act of 1997, the Roth IRA, often called simply a "Roth," ushered in a new era in the tax structure of retirement plans. Rather than deferring taxes until a distribution is taken, you can now eliminate taxation completely. Contributions are not deductible, but distributions should be tax free. Taxes on investment returns are not deferred but eliminated, due to payment of income taxes up front on the contributions.

Roth owners are unique, in that they are not subject to required minimum distributions. Money does not ever have to come out of the Roth IRA over the account owner's lifetime or the remaining spouse's lifetime. There is no required beginning date, and, with a Roth, you can continue to make contributions after age 70½ as long as you qualify.

That said, a Roth is not for everyone, and there are restrictions as to who can utilize this investment tool. After the Roth owner's death, if the beneficiary is a non-spouse (child, grandchild, etc.), withdrawals become mandatory. Beneficiaries are subject to RMDs, but with proper planning those RMDs can be tax-free.

> ## HORSE SENSE
>
> The biggest downside to a Roth is the mental road block that tells us to put off paying taxes as long as possible. While this sentiment is generally true, if paying taxes now will produce enhanced benefits later, you have to overcome your aversion to taxes—at least temporarily! By paying tax now, rather than later, you will pay 0% tax on generations of qualified withdrawals. We don't know about you but we like the 0% tax bracket!

To review, with a Roth, you pay taxes on any money being contributed, and, later, you get your principal and growth tax-free. There is no required beginning date on distributions, so there are no required minimum distributions while you are alive, and no maximum age for making contributions as long as you qualify! You may participate in a Roth as well as a company sponsored retirement plan. Not only are we trying to shelter your money from taxes for as long as possible with the stretch concept, we also want to shelter your money as much as possible from any tax.

You may make nondeductible contributions to a Roth IRA as long as you have earned income. This is a way for the IRS to restrict who may participate. These contributions are referred to as regular contributions—we suspect to differentiate between those and some kind of irregular contributions. In 2008 and beyond, the maximum allowable contribution to a Roth IRA is $5,000 per individual, per year, with a "catch-up" provision. The catch-up provision allows those age 50 and over to contribute an additional $1,000 in 2011 for a total of $6,000.

Not everyone qualifies to make contributions, and those who do must be able to afford this plan. Maximum contributions for any year are for all IRAs: traditional and Roth. You cannot contribute

$5,000 to each; the $5,000 limit is an aggregate limit. Keep in mind that contributions to SEPs and SIMPLE IRAs are NOT treated as IRA contributions, so you may contribute to a traditional IRA or Roth in addition.

Income Limits

The IRS has set income limitations to contribute to a Roth. Single taxpayers with an **adjusted gross income** (AGI) up to $105,000 can make a full contribution. Married taxpayers filing *jointly* are limited to a maximum of up to $167,000. Married taxpayers filing *separately* cannot utilize the Roth unless they have lived apart from each other for the entire year. The maximum allowable contributions are not all-or-none propositions. There are also phase-out levels for AGI. Contributions for single taxpayers are phased-out starting at $105,000 and they cannot make a contribution if their adjusted gross income is in excess of $120,000. Contributions for married taxpayers filing jointly are phased-out starting at $167,000 and they cannot make a contribution if their adjusted gross income is in excess of $177,000. If your tax filing status is "married filing separately" (and you live with your spouse) you cannot make a Roth IRA contribution if your AGI is in excess of $10,000.

Like traditional IRA contributions, Roth contributions can be made until April 15th following the year in question. IRAs must be funded with cash contributions only; no other assets, such as securities, are allowed to fuel Roth IRAs.

HORSE SENSE

If your contributions to a Roth are reduced due to exceeding the income limitations, consider contributing the remaining allowable amount to a traditional IRA.

Converting to a Roth

The second way to fund a Roth is by **converting**, the process of transferring funds from a traditional IRA into a Roth. The dollar amount converted is included in your gross income. Therefore, converting becomes a taxable event. There is no ceiling on the amount you may convert in any one year. Despite the IRS terminology, converting should be looked at as a process, not an event. Pieces of a traditional IRA can be converted over time. So, a traditional IRA can be converted a little bit at a time, over many years, or in one fell swoop. The conversion must be done with *same* (or like) property. So, if you roll over and receive cash, you must contribute cash to the Roth. If your rollover includes stock, you must contribute the stock to the Roth. To be efficient from a taxpaying point of view, work with a CPA or another knowledgeable advisor who will tell you what conversion strategy is best.

The problem with Roth IRAs lies in the upfront tax bill due when converting. We must look past the fear of paying taxes today. This is especially true when paying today could mean much less overall owed tax. Consider what you and your beneficiaries will pay over time on the growth of a traditional IRA, which is taxed when distributed. With a Roth, you eliminate the tax that will be due on the growth of the account over your lifetime, your spouse's lifetime, and the lifetime of your heirs. Remember, there are no RMDs with the Roth, so no money must be distributed if it isn't needed. The Roth is especially attractive to people who

DON'T TRIP UP!

Be careful not to push your tax bracket substantially higher through a conversion.

do not plan on requiring the money in the account for their own income during retirement.

You will pay the same amount of estate tax on a $1,000,000 traditional IRA as you will with a $1,000,000 Roth IRA, but you eliminate income tax problems when you employ the Roth method. Because of this, the Roth will mean more to your heirs.

Do not convert to a Roth IRA if you cannot pay due taxes with non-IRA dollars. Pay the tax with money outside of your retirement accounts! As with most rules, there are occasional exceptions to the "pay with money outside the plan" rule. One exception is a wealthy person with almost all of her wealth held in a very large IRA.

Conversion Options

How do the logistics of converting a traditional IRA to a Roth IRA work? There are four popular paths:

1. Take distribution from a traditional IRA, and then roll those dollars to the Roth.
2. Make a plan to plan transfer from the traditional IRA custodian to the Roth IRA custodian.
3. If the custodian will remain the same, **redesignate** the traditional IRA to a Roth IRA. Redesignating simply changes the title of the IRA, making it a Roth, but you still have to complete the Roth paperwork.
4. If eligible for a plan distribution, convert your employer plan funds to a Roth.

Conversion Rules

In cases where investors are over age 70½, prior to making a conversion they must first take the RMD from a traditional IRA if they are subject to minimum distributions. RMDs cannot be rolled to a Roth. The first dollars distributed from a traditional IRA each year are considered RMDs until the full required amount is taken. Roth distributions do not qualify as RMDs from a traditional IRA.

Converting a distribution from a traditional IRA will be treated by the IRS as a regular contribution, and could be subject to an excess contribution penalty, if it is in excess of the applicable limit on regular Roth contributions. The penalty will be imposed annually until the excess contribution is taken out of the Roth.

Converting Non-Taxable Money to a Roth

A conversion from a traditional IRA to a Roth is considered a distribution of the converted amount for income tax purposes. This amount converted is included in gross income, unless part of the converted amount is a return of your basis. The proportion of converted money representing basis in the traditional IRA is not taxable.

FROM THE HORSE'S MOUTH

Your traditional IRA is worth $100,000 and you have made a total of $10,000 of non-deductible contributions to the traditional IRA over time. You have not taken any distributions from the account and you converted the entire account to a Roth in 2005. You only include $90,000 in gross income from the conversion ($100,000 total value minus $10,000 in basis).

Multiple IRAs and Cream in the Coffee Basis

What if you have multiple traditional IRAs, some funded with after-tax contributions, and others with an initial contribution or basis but that were not deductible? If you want to convert any of these into Roths, the amount of the conversion that is considered a distribution for income tax purposes can be confusing. Instead of figuring out the amount on an IRA by IRA basis, the

IRS deems any conversions from any of your traditional IRAs to have come proportionately from all of your IRAs. Let's look at an example.

Your traditional IRA is worth $50,000; your contributions of $10,000 were not deductible. You also have a rollover IRA worth $200,000 which contains no after-tax contributions. You want to do a Roth conversion for the $50,000 traditional IRA. The initial thought is to subtract your $10,000 in basis from the total value and pay taxes on the $40,000 difference ... *Except*, that is wrong. Here is how we calculate the taxable amount in this conversion.

Take your non-deductible basis of $10,000, and divide by the total value of all your IRAs at the end of the prior year ($250,000). This comes out to 4% (.04). Multiply this by the amount you are converting (the $50,000 traditional IRA) to determine the proportionate basis in the conversion that is not taxable: 4% multiplied by $50,000 = $2,000 (the nontaxable amount). Subtract the nontaxable amount from the amount that you are converting to get the taxable amount ($50,000 minus $2,000 = $48,000). The remaining basis in the $50,000 traditional IRA is $8,000; it "waits" to be used when you convert some or all of the other IRA (the rollover IRA of $200,000).

This interesting accounting has been called the "cream in the coffee" analogy. Once the cream has been poured into the coffee there is no way to remove just the cream or just the coffee. By choosing to *not* convert every traditional IRA to a Roth, the taxpayer is forced to spread any existing basis over any distribution, eliminating creative conversion strategies designed to finesse taxes due. In other words, any conversions are deemed to come proportionately from all the taxpayer's traditional IRAs, even if it came from only one, and even if that IRA was funded totally with after-tax dollars.

Putting It in Perspective

1987 was the first year non-deductible contributions were permitted for IRAs. When making a non-deductible contribution, you are required to report that contribution on Form 8606 (which is attached to the 1040). Form 8606 should detail the cumulative total of such contributions. In theory, to determine your basis in your traditional IRAs, you need to look no further than your most recent form 8606. We say that this is in theory because many who should have filed this form never do!

Non-taxable and taxable money can be rolled over to a traditional IRA. Once the non-taxable dollars are rolled to a traditional IRA from a qualified retirement plan, these dollars are well positioned to be converted to a Roth. As an example, some

FROM THE HORSE'S MOUTH

*Joan retired from Company A in 2004 and rolled her qualified plan money into her traditional IRA. The IRA had some after-tax contributions in it. Therefore, the IRA has **basis** (money that would not be taxed upon distribution), plus monies that would be taxable when distributed. In 2005, Joan started her own business and also created a retirement plan for the business. At this point, Joan rolled her IRA into her company-sponsored retirement plan. IRS rules dictate that only pre-tax money can be rolled into a qualified plan, so the only funds left in the IRA after the rollover are the original after-tax contributions, which have basis and are therefore tax-free when distributed. Since this is Joan's first year at her new venture, her income is below the $100,000 Roth IRA conversion limit, so she converts the entire balance of the traditional IRA to a Roth. The result is no taxation at conversion, because 100% of the converted funds are nontaxable. No cream in the coffee problem, and Joan and her heirs will enjoy tax-free growth potential over their lifetimes.*

retirees have after-tax contributions in their company's retirement plan. By first rolling their plan into a traditional IRA, then converting the after-tax funds to a Roth, they very efficiently get the advantages of the Roth.

Are you confused, since we just discussed the cream in the coffee problem? Wondering how to avoid this scenario? It is not easy, but there is a way. First, roll the plan into a traditional IRA. Then, go back to work for a company with a retirement plan (or start your own plan if you are self employed—as a consultant, for example), and roll the pre-tax portion of your IRA into the company's plan. Qualified plans will not accept after-tax dollars into the plan so all that is left in the IRA are the after-tax monies. The money left in your IRA can now be converted to a Roth without any taxation because the conversion is made up entirely of after-tax dollars that won't be taxed again when converted.

The 10% premature distribution penalty does not apply if a conversion occurs while payments are being received as part of a 72(t) schedule, so long as the payments continue from the Roth IRA. A conversion will *not* be treated as a distribution that modifies the series of equal payments. Again, this is true as long as distributions continue from the Roth. If you do not continue the series from the Roth, the series will be considered modified. If this occurs within five years of the first payment or the individual is under 59½, the taxpayer will be subject to recapture tax. The moral of this story is to continue with your payments after conversion!

Estate Planning

Individuals often convert to a Roth for estate planning purposes, and to maximize the inheritance to their children. Converting to a Roth reduces estate taxes, because the tax paid on a conversion reduces the taxable estate. Elvis fans might say that "the money has left the building." By the way, had Elvis lived, he would have reached his RBD in 2005!

Age is often the catalyst to start the estate planning process. By converting to a Roth, you can get the government to pay a portion of your conversion tax! Older taxpayers (or, as we prefer to call them, the chronologically gifted), or the ill, who are also wealthy enough to be subject to estate tax should consider this plan of action.

Convert the traditional IRA to a Roth as shown in the following example: Let's look at a $500,000 IRA which is converted. Roughly $200,000 in tax is paid since the owner is in the highest combined state and federal tax bracket. At death, the estate will be subject to estate taxes in the ballpark of 40%. The $200,000 that was paid in income tax due to the Roth conversion is no longer in the estate so roughly $80,000 has been saved in estate tax. Through the conversion, hasn't the government subsidized the Roth conversion nearly 60/40 through lost estate tax revenue? The government effectively subsidized 40% of the $200,000 income taxes that you paid (or $80,000) by the estate taxes that were eliminated by converting to a Roth. And, the heirs have a $500,000 Roth IRA that they can withdraw from tax-free.

Recharacterizing

What if you convert to a Roth, pay the tax, then realize your financial situation has changed, and maybe you can't afford to pay the taxes due to the conversion? Or, what if your account balance drops? Luckily, you have the opportunity to use a "get out of jail free card" from the IRS—called a **recharacterization**. If you convert to a Roth, and *for any reason* you want to undo the conversion, the IRS allows you to do so, and back out of the tax bill.

HORSE SENSE

With the ability to recharacterize, there is no risk in converting to a Roth. However, remember to perform any changes within the allowed time frame. Your heirs can even recharacterize after your death if they deem it necessary. Just be aware of the IRS recharacterization rules.

There are some rules involved with recharacterizing—there are always rules. You surely know that by now!

1. The recharacterization must be via a trustee-to-trustee transfer, not a rollover. A rollover would require a distribution followed by a recontribution.
2. There are time limits to undo the conversion. The deadline to recharacterize is the due date of the tax return for the year of the contribution plus extensions.

Let's consider a recharacterization in 2005. You have until October 15, 2006 to recharacterize. October 15 is the due date for filing a tax return when extensions are used. Enlist the help of a CPA if you find yourself wanting to recharacterize. There are some details that may have to be included on your return if you are filing for an extension to recharacterize.

FROM THE HORSE'S MOUTH . . .

Let's say you convert your $100,000 IRA to a Roth, but unfortunately, you invested in the next WorldCom or Enron. With this teetering corporate scandal, share prices plummet. The value of your account drops to $10,000. You can cry "uncle" to the IRS and undo the conversion. If you have already paid the income tax, you will get a refund of tax paid.

Inherited Roth IRAs

You inherit a Roth IRA and you are now in the driver's seat for years of tax-free stretching. HOORAY! In our example, however, due to an investment catastrophe, the inherited Roth has dropped in value, significantly, with no likely chance of recovery. Good news: within time limits, the beneficiary can end the Roth and recharacterize to get a tax refund.

Here's an example. Your mother converts $200,000 to a Roth in early 2004, and then dies unexpectedly in November 2004. You were named the beneficiary of the Roth, but unfortunately, the value has dropped to $10,000. Your mother has already paid tax on a $200,000 account but, due to investment losses, the value her tax was based on no longer exists. You may recharacterize the inherited Roth back to a traditional IRA, and receive a refund of the tax that your mother paid at conversion. This is what is called a contested issue, and a Private Letter Ruling may be necessary. Before you begin this transaction, it is advised that you consult the IRS, to confirm that the recharacterization will work the way you intend it to. In this situation, it is most likely in your best interest to use a financial advisor, who will walk you through the process of contacting the IRS.

HORSE SENSE

Conversions are often a multi-year process rather than a one-time event. Pieces of a traditional IRA can be converted over a period of years for tax planning purposes. So, each year that a partial conversion is done, keep that Roth separate from other Roth money until the time limit for recharacterizing has expired (October 15 of the next year). By doing so, you give yourself the ability to only recharacterize that portion of the overall Roth assets.

To Convert or Not

We all know the Roth sounds great—tax-free income is a good thing whichever way you slice it. And we could all use a little more of a good thing. But, is it worth paying taxes upfront, when your money could have stayed in a traditional IRA until it is distributed? This is the big question investors must tackle. Is it more efficient to pay taxes now and get the tax-free distributions later, or should you stay put in the traditional IRA, and continue to defer taxes until funds are distributed?

Here we refer you to some wise advice: remember that mathematics is your friend. We prefer to use software programs which develop simulations to help us answer the "convert or leave be" question. These programs allow us to manipulate the data, and to analyze multiple scenarios for each client. There is no magic here, and the numbers show us that. If you take $100 and pay the income tax at a 20% bracket, then deposit the proceeds into a Roth which earns 8% per year for 20 years, and withdraw the money, you will have the same amount of money as if you kept the $100 in a traditional IRA, earned 8% per year for 20 years and withdrew the money at a 20% tax bracket. As you probably already realize, at least one factor in the equation (your tax rate, the number of years, current interest rates) must change for the Roth approach to be profitable.

So, why do so many people convert to Roths? One very common reason, and, in our opinion, the biggest advantage of a Roth, is the elimination of RMDs. Because Roths have no required minimum distributions, money is allowed to stay in the Roth longer than with a traditional IRA. The tax-free compounding can continue to a greater extent with the Roth over the account owner's lifetime, since no money is forced out. If the spouse is beneficiary of the Roth, she

DON'T TRIP UP!

When an inherited Roth IRA is recharacterized, it becomes a traditional IRA, and it can never be converted to a Roth again. However, a Roth IRA that is not inherited and is recharacterized, can be converted to a Roth again. Recharacterizations are limited to one per year.

can roll the Roth over to her name and continue with the tax-free compounding without RMDs over her lifetime as well. The Roth doesn't require RMDs to begin until it is inherited by a non-spouse beneficiary. *The passage of time magnifies the advantage of a Roth.* If the funds in the Roth can be left to grow over an additional twenty or thirty years without being diminished by RMDs (as they would in a traditional IRA), the Roth becomes a clear winner.

DON'T TRIP UP!

Make sure to note that a required distribution from a Roth cannot be counted as satisfying a RMD from any other kind of IRA.

Maximizing Roth Potential

To benefit from the no RMD requirement, you must have sufficient assets and/or income to live on outside of the Roth, so the Roth is allowed to grow untouched. Maximize the Roth potential by planning to eventually leave the Roth to younger beneficiaries; they can take withdrawals over their longer life expectancy to maximize the stretch. But make sure that you have the assets to pay the income tax due upon conversion with non-IRA assets. There should also be ample non-Roth assets to pay any potential estate tax that may be due at the Roth owner's death so the Roth isn't used for tax bills.

Conversion Problems

One client recently said, "All this sounds great, if I plan on pinching every penny in retirement and not enjoying the fruits of my labor. But that isn't going to happen. I want to enjoy myself and my money!" We agree with him. It is your money. After all those years of work, you have earned the right to some fun. It is not your job to make everyone around you rich, and any planning should always start with you, the IRA owner, in the forefront.

After many, many meetings with a wide variety of investors, we've come to realize something: despite years of scrimping and saving, it's not always easy to realize that you've accumulated more money than you and your spouse will ever need. So, try to think of the big picture. If you aren't going to spend every last nickel you have, let's get it to your heirs in the most advantageous way possible!

FROM THE HORSE'S MOUTH

Let's say the only asset you have left when you die is your Roth IRA, which has a $50,000 balance. What could that really be worth for your granddaughter? She has a 70 year life expectancy, and will earn 8% interest over her lifetime. What is that worth in real terms? Let's take a look: How about $330 per month tax free, forever? Now, $330 a month doesn't do much today but think of how far it could go towards books and board at college, payment for a new car, contribution to rent, or a cushion for the first mortgage! That is how we recommend that you think—in terms of the "Grandpa IRA."

Money Smart IRA Ideas

Here are three ideas—do any of them make sense for your family? If they do, your heirs will thank you!

1. Your children or grandchildren have after school jobs, or have earned a small income, but are still in a low tax bracket. Make a gift to them in the form of a Roth contribution. What could a few thousand dollars per year for the next twenty years be worth to little Allison? A lot!

2. Put Grandma on the payroll for her work watching and educating the grandchildren. That earned income makes her eligible for Roth contributions. Help Grandma with the taxes of a Roth conversion of her IRA. If it is eventually going to the grandkids anyway, why not pay the conversion tax at Grandma's bracket for years of tax-free growth potential and tax-free distributions that won't be taxed at your bracket?

3. If the ultimate beneficiaries of your IRA are the kids or grandkids, and those beneficiaries are already in the highest tax brackets, why not take more than your RMD to the lower income tax bracket limit and convert that to a Roth? When you pass away, your retirement money won't be eroded by your beneficiary's high tax bracket, because they will receive tax-free income. Convert pieces of your IRA each year up to the limit for remaining in the lower tax brackets to give the kids in the highest tax brackets tax-free distributions. In addition to paying taxes now at the lower bracket, the children will also avoid the paperwork hassle associated with the IRD deduction (which we'll discuss later) when they file their own tax returns.

Getting Money Out of the Roth IRA

Let's recap some of nuances involved with distributing money out of a Roth:

1. Because there are no RMDs with a Roth, money is never forced out of the IRA over the account owner's lifetime, or the spousal beneficiary's lifetime.

2. Voluntary withdrawals or RMDs for non-spouse beneficiaries who inherit a Roth *should* be tax-free. We say should be because there is always a catch with the IRS. For a distribution to be tax-free, it has to be considered a "qualified distribution."

3. Qualified distributions are always tax free and not includable in gross income for the IRS regardless of whether the recipient is the participant or a beneficiary.

4. The principal can always be taken out of a Roth tax free. You've already paid the tax!

5. When taking money out of a Roth, the original principal is taken first, then your growth or appreciation comes out when the principal is gone. This type of accounting (called **FIFO**—first-in-first-out) allows you to minimize taxes if you distribute the money over time.

Rules for qualified distributions:

1. The distribution is made after a five year waiting period and:
   - The participant is at least 59½
   - The distribution is made after the participant dies
   - The participant is mentally or physically totally disabled or the distribution is a qualified special purpose distribution (first time home purchase, etc.)

How does the five year waiting period work? The waiting period begins on January 1 of the first year a contribution was made to any Roth. For example, if you make a contribution to a Roth in August 2003, your five-year period began January 1, 2003. You could have taken a qualified distribution in 2008 as long as you were over age 59½. You actually have until April 15 after the year you want to make a contribution for—exactly like a traditional IRA contribution.

HORSE SENSE

Any contributions subsequent to your initial contribution (into the same or different Roth account) do not start a new five year period. Therefore, it can be a very smart strategy to convert a small amount of any traditional IRA into a Roth, to start the five year clock ticking.

Nonqualified Distributions

Even if a Roth distribution is not qualified, it still receives favorable tax treatment versus a traditional IRA distribution. Regular Roth contributions or conversions have already been taxed, and will not be taxed again upon distribution. Contributions and converted money equal the Roth owner's basis. When the account grows, that growth is the part that has not yet been taxed. Whether the growth is ever taxed depends on meeting the five year threshold and whether or not a distribution is a qualified distribution. The Roth can hold both taxed and non-taxed money. So, distributions come out of a Roth in a specific order according to the IRS. The first dollars withdrawn come from basis in the Roth. They are contributions and converted funds that have already been taxed.

Let's review an example. You contribute to a Roth, but need money before the five year period. The first dollars out come from your basis so no tax is due. You may take out every penny of your basis and owe no tax. This is an example of a non-qualified distribution that still comes out tax free. This is far more efficient than the treatment distributions get from traditional IRAs. Remember the cream in the coffee analogy. All distributions come out proportionately from the basis and earnings within all of the participant's IRAs. Traditional IRA basis is recovered over time, as more and more money comes out of the IRA.

Ordering Rules

The sequence of money coming out of the Roth is determined by the **Ordering Rules**:

1. Distributions come from all contributions first.
2. If a Roth has both contributions and converted funds from a traditional IRA, the regular contributions come out first, then the converted funds.
3. When contributions are withdrawn, and funds converted from a traditional IRA are being used for withdrawals, the portion of the conversion that has already been taxed comes out first, then the non-taxable money last if there is any.

4. When the only money left in the Roth is the growth of the contributions and converted funds, it finally comes out. If you have not held the Roth for five years and are under 59½, the growth will be taxable and you will be subject to the IRA 10% early withdrawal penalty.

HORSE SENSE

When you need to determine if a nonqualified distribution is taxable, just go down the list for the Ordering Rules. Your original contributions can always be withdrawn tax-free.

Roth Distribution Under Age 59½

If you are under age 59½ and convert from a traditional to a Roth IRA, you must first pay the tax due with taxable funds, not IRA funds. Otherwise, you will be subject to the 10% early withdrawal penalty for the funds withdrawn but not converted. If you then take a Roth distribution under the age of 59½, and you haven't held the account for five years, you will be subject to another 10% penalty. Each conversion has its own five-year holding period.

Spousal Rollover

If a spouse is the beneficiary of a Roth IRA, she can roll her specified share, up to 100%, into her own Roth IRA. As owner of the Roth, her age will dictate applicable tax rules. She becomes the full owner, no longer just the beneficiary. Therefore, she is not required to take any RMDs.

Let's look at an example of spousal rollover. At age 50, Mr. Lee converts $100,000 in August 2004 (his five year period begins as of January 1, 2004 and ends January 1, 2009). He dies in 2005, leaving Mrs. Lee as beneficiary. She is only 40 years-old in 2005. Mrs. Lee, against the advice of her financial advisor, rolls her husband's Roth into a new Roth in her name. In 2006, Mrs. Lee withdraws the entire account—which has grown to $120,000 ($100,000 worth of converted funds plus $20,000 in growth). Bad move! Unfortunately, the distribution is not a qualified one, since the five year period has not been fulfilled. Taxes are now due on the $20,000 in growth and there is a 10% penalty of $12,000 on the entire $120,000 balance because she is under the *magical* age 59½.

Instead of a spousal rollover in the above example, let's discuss what might have been a better decision. Mrs. Lee remains a beneficiary of her inherited Roth IRA, and empties the account in 2006. She escapes the early withdrawal penalty because she is not the owner, but the beneficiary. She will owe taxes on the $20,000 of growth because the five year period has not been fulfilled so it is a non-qualified distribution. This scenario is an improvement over the first.

The best scenario for Mrs. Lee is to remain a beneficiary, withdraw up to the $100,000 that was conversion money so it is not taxable, and wait until 2009 to take the remainder of the account. Even if the balance of the account has grown to $200,000 by then, the distribution would be qualified and tax-free because it has been held for five years.

Non-Spousal Beneficiaries

We know there are no RMDs for the Roth owner or the spouse beneficiary. However, once the Roth is inherited by a non-spouse, minimum distribution rules will begin, like it or not. Because there is no RBD for a Roth, distributions are calculated by following the minimum distribution rules as if a) the Roth owner instead had a traditional IRA, and b) died before his RBD. This is regardless of the actual age of the Roth owner at death.

All right! You made it this far in the book! We'll move onto the next chapter, where we tackle tribulations unique to taxpayers who may have long-term care concerns and/or are wealthy enough to have estate tax issues.

NOTES

NOTES

CHAPTER 7

THE FINISH LINE: ESTATE PLANNING FOR LARGE IRAS

S o far, we've explored IRA distribution planning without factor-ing in the impact of estate taxes. While we're talking about your money, we again want to reiterate that the primary goal of having accumulated money in a retirement plan is to enjoy life according to your desires and circumstances. It *is* possible to be too much in love with income tax deferral and planning the transfer of your wealth. After all, isn't watching a sunset from a cozy beach chair more fun than admiring your IRA statement?

Nonetheless, there are many people who, even after spending what they deem appropriate, find themselves with more money than the government allows under the estate tax exemption. That means that the federal government will impose the estate or death tax. This chapter is specifically for those IRA owners who will be subject to estate tax at death.

> ## DON'T TRIP UP!
>
> *Don't make the mistake so many people do, and underestimate the size of your estate! You can't just add up the value of your assets today. Instead, think what they will be worth in 5, 10 or 20 years. And don't forget any possible inheritances you may receive. Refer to the IRS website (www.irs.gov) in the estate and gift tax section for up-to-date estate tax rules and regulations. Publication 590 explains estate and gift tax topics for IRAs.*

If your estate, including your retirement accounts, will be subject to estate tax, your beneficiaries will need adequate financial resources to pay the bill. We want to make sure that any tax paid does not come from retirement dollars. Why? Taxes, that's why! Hefty IRAs are an easy target for income and estate taxes. The usual strategy to reduce estate taxes—minimizing the taxable estate by making gifts—is difficult and potentially problematic with IRAs. Why? Because you cannot give away parts of an IRA to reduce future estate taxes without first taking a distribution, which creates a taxable event.

If one dollar is needed from an IRA to pay estate tax, you will have to withdraw that dollar plus additional money for the income tax that will be triggered from the IRA distribution. Therefore, you won't just withdraw one dollar out of the IRA; you will have to take $1.20-$1.30 depending on your tax bracket. This can cause a downward spiral which threatens to implode an IRA. The question on every large IRA owner's mind should be how to reduce RMDs and impending estate taxes without sacrificing the total benefits and cash flow for the family. Unfortunately, with IRAs there is no magic button or Holy Grail.

Estate Tax Exemption

Every taxpayer gets a federal estate tax exemption, which increased to $5 million in 2011. Referred to as the **credit shelter**, this amount is the dollar level of assets that are protected by the estate exemption at death. Since each person is allowed the exemption, a married couple is allowed $5 million in exemptions for each spouse. The problem with this scenario is that, unless someone has experience in estate planning, the first exemption is usually wasted.

When the first spouse dies, leaving all assets to the surviving spouse, the exemption that the deceased spouse had is lost forever. The $5 million of assets that could've been sheltered is now subject to estate taxation. A spouse can leave an unlimited amount of property to another without any taxation, but in doing so, one credit shelter amount goes away and cannot be recouped by the surviving spouse. In other words, Spouse A dies and leaves everything to Spouse B. At Spouse B's death, only one credit shelter remains—whether Spouse A used his or not. If the credit shelter isn't used by the first spouse, its benefits are lost forever.

Unlimited Marital Deduction

The IRS isn't concerned about assets passing from one spouse to the next; they know their pay day will come eventually, at the death of the second spouse. All too often the government collects more at the death of the second spouse because one exemption wasn't utilized. The title "Unlimited Marital Deduction" falsely leads people to believe they are eliminating estate taxes on their death, but, unfortunately, they are not. Instead, they are merely postponing estate taxes, which will be paid by subsequent heirs. Remember that the government is going to tax those future dollars.

Properly setting up your estate is the first step to making sure each spouse can utilize his or her own estate tax exemption. The exemption is only valid if you leave an estate to a beneficiary other than your spouse.

Non-Spouse Beneficiary

A spouse is usually the beneficiary of the IRA if you don't expect estate taxes to be an issue. Problems arise when substantial IRAs and other assets in the estate will be subject to estate taxation. One option is to leave some of the IRA (up to the GST limit) to a non-spouse beneficiary—the children or grandchildren, for instance. This will allow the IRA owner to use some or all of his exemption, get that portion of the IRA out of the surviving spouse's estate, and allow the beneficiaries to stretch 100% of the IRA over their life expectancies. OK, but don't get excited! We aren't going to disinherit the spouse and leave her out in the cold! Keep reading!

If there are sufficient assets for the spouse to live comfortably, leaving some or all of an IRA to a non-spouse beneficiary is the most efficient means of reducing potential estate taxes. This is a better strategy than leaving everything to the spouse, who then leaves the IRA to the beneficiaries. In this case, one exemption is wasted, and the IRA has time to grow inside the surviving spouse's estate, causing an eventual increase in estate taxation. The problem with the strategy of leaving some IRA money to a non-spouse beneficiary is the loss of control over the asset; it now belongs to someone else. If losing control doesn't sit well, there is another option: the credit shelter trust.

A less efficient but still attractive method of avoiding some estate tax is to create a **Credit Shelter Trust**. The trust can be funded while the IRA owner is alive or at his death. The trust is funded up to the allowable exemption amount. Any remaining assets above the exemption limit pass directly to the heirs.

This type of trust is called a Credit Shelter Trust because the federal estate tax exemption is actually an estate tax credit. The trust is designed to capture the exemption—hence the term "Shelter" Trust. Since the exemption number is a moving target from year to year, the trust is written to be funded with the exemption amount at the time of death. The surviving spouse is the beneficiary of the trust, but does not have unlimited control over it; this makes certain that the trust money is not included in the surviving spouse's estate. The assets in the trust escape estate tax on the first spouse's estate, because it was sheltered by the amount of the spouse's unified credit. These assets will not be taxed in the surviving spouse's estate because she does not own the trust.

HORSE SENSE

The drawback of a Credit Shelter Trust is the common downside of most strategies to reduce estate taxes: loss of control. In this case, the loss falls on the surviving spouse, who loses some control of the assets inside the trust.

When a credit shelter trust is used, the surviving spouse remains as beneficiary of the trust assets. Therefore, she can take distributions from the trust, but the trust property is legally owned by the trust for tax purposes. The remaining beneficiaries, usually the children, receive any property still remaining in the trust at the death of the second spouse. In addition to income from the trust, most Credit Shelter Trusts are now drafted to allow for the invasion of principal by the spouse for health needs, education, maintenance, and support. The wording allows the spouse to access the principal for almost any reason, as long as the money is truly needed. Taking a distribution from the trust to let the money sit in your money market is not a necessity, and could cause a problem.

The most attractive features of the trust mirror those of outright gifting to a non-spouse beneficiary: a) utilizing the estate exemption, and b) allowing for estate tax-free growth of the assets, since they will not be included in the surviving spouse's estate. The Credit Shelter Trust will not save any estate tax that could not have been saved through an outright gift or bequest to a non-spouse. Naming your children as beneficiaries of an IRA worth $1 million makes use of the estate exemption just as the trust does.

DON'T TRIP UP!

A Credit Shelter Trust is an **irrevocable trust**. This mean that once funded, it is for all intents and purposes impossible to undo. This kind of trust is great for estate planning purposes, but it might be a problem if the spouse needs nursing home care, and wants to qualify for Medicaid's long-term care benefits. In some states, the Credit Shelter Trust principal is required to be used first before eligibility for Medicaid benefits, and cannot be transferred to a healthy relative, for example. If this is a consideration, seek the advice of a competent elder law attorney.

The difference is that the trust allows for some control of the assets by the surviving spouse. If control is not a key factor, don't waste your energy with a trust.

If your IRA is over the current $5 million exemption, consider splitting the IRA into multiple IRAs with different beneficiaries named on each. Leave up to $5 million to the children or the trust, with the remainder going to the spouse, which will pass tax-free under the unlimited marital deduction.

For *very* large estates made up primarily of an IRA, it might prove beneficial to take a distribution from the IRA to fund the Credit Shelter Trust. The IRA owner pays the income tax and funds the trust with after-tax dollars. This strategy sacrifices income tax deferral in the interest of greater estate tax savings. If the IRA owner is approaching his RBD and the RMDs are going to be enormous anyway, or if the IRA owner is terminally ill, for example, he will have peace of mind knowing that the trust has been funded.

Drawbacks

When a Credit Shelter Trust is exercised, generally distributions will begin within one year of the IRA owner's death. Compare this to the situation where the IRA was left directly to the spouse, who rolled over the IRA. In this case, distributions could be postponed until the surviving spouse reached the required beginning date (70½). If the spouse remained as a beneficiary of the IRA, distributions could be postponed until the IRA owner would have reached the required beginning date.

IRA funds paid to the trust will be distributed over the life expectancy of the oldest beneficiary, who is usually the spouse. This is unfavorable for the other beneficiaries, who may have much longer life expectancies, and could therefore stretch the remaining IRA funds over a longer period of time. After the spouse dies, the remaining beneficiaries get the short end of the stick again, as they have to continue the payment schedule the spouse was on when receiving distributions. Therefore, the stretch gets shortened again.

Non-IRA assets are the best choice to fund a Credit Shelter Trust. But if the IRA is the only asset, and it is large enough to trigger estate taxes at the death of the second spouse, funding the trust with IRA money is better than doing nothing!

DON'T TRIP UP!

Do not fund a Credit Shelter Trust with a Roth IRA. If this is done, the life expectancy of the oldest beneficiary, usually the spouse, is used to calculate RMDs. Instead, leave the Roth directly to your spouse, so she can perform a rollover. Then the money will not be subject to RMDs until her death, when her beneficiaries begin the distributions.

Funding the credit shelter trust with a Roth greatly reduces the amount of time of tax-free growth and tax-free distributions one enjoys, after already paying income taxes for the Roth conversion. You have paid the price for generations of tax-free growth followed by tax-free distributions but your beneficiaries won't get to benefit from it.

Let us repeat: IRA planning should be viewed as a *process*, not an event. The key is having the knowledge to implement how you want your assets distributed and passing that information on to your beneficiaries. If you are unsure if a trust is appropriate, name your spouse as the primary beneficiary and the trust as contingent beneficiary. If, at your death, the best strategy is for the IRA to go to the trust, your spouse can disclaim the IRA and it will pass to the trust as the next beneficiary in line.

Disclaiming and Estate Planning

A **disclaimer** is the refusal to accept a gift of inherited property. Disclaiming allows estate planning to occur even after the IRA owner's death. It is not recommended that all estate planning occur after death, but through the use of disclaiming one can gain flexibility and control. Family members can run the numbers, and wait to make crucial decisions and changes at a more optimal time. Once the owner has passed away, we better understand the exact account balances, the overall financial situation, and needs of beneficiaries.

In the case of disclaiming a retirement plan, the primary beneficiary states that she does not want to inherit the IRA. The IRA custodian then looks at the beneficiary agreement for the contingent beneficiary. The contingent beneficiary will become the primary beneficiary, as if in a case where the disclaimant predeceased the original account owner. Even though the disclaimant voluntarily parts with the right to some form of money, the disclaimant has not made a gift for gift tax purposes. Therefore, this is not considered a taxable event.

Disclaimers get too little respect. While disclaiming can be very effective for planning purposes, the papers must always be drafted very carefully. For a disclaimer to be acknowledged by the IRS, it must be a **qualified disclaimer**. To be a qualified disclaimer, it must:

1. Be irrevocable, unconditional, and in writing.

2. Be presented to the person making the gift, if alive. If deceased, a disclaimer must be presented to the deceased's legal representative, to the company holding legal title to the property or to the person in possession of the property, and to the state government. The onus is on the disclaimant to determine who must receive the written disclaimer.

3. Be presented within nine months of the original transfer of the property.

In the event the transfer is due to the death of a spouse, the date of death is when the clock starts ticking. Don't get confused about the timeline. It is nine months, unlike the required minimum distribution time line that allows until September 30 of the year after the IRA owner died to identify the designated beneficiary. RMD rules do not apply to the disclaimer time frame.

4. The disclaimant must not have accepted the property being disclaimed or any benefit from it. Examples of acceptance include:
   • Cashing a dividend check from a stock you are disclaiming
   • Accepting a bond interest payment
   • Buying or selling securities
   • Accepting something in exchange for the disclaimed asset—cash or barter
   • Acceptance requires an action by the beneficiary for example, naming a successor beneficiary

Being named on an account does not constitute acceptance. For example, consider if monthly payments were automatically sent from John Smith's IRA to his joint checking account with his wife Martha. When John dies, the IRA custodian continues to send monthly distributions to the checking account. In this case, Martha has not accepted any benefit. However, once the custodian is aware of John's death and the distributions cease, Martha should be careful that the balance of the checking account does not dip below the total amount of distributions sent to the checking account after John died. If the balance does dip below and Martha tries to disclaim John's IRA, the IRS may block her disclaimer. This is an extreme example but you get the picture; you can't take any benefit whatsoever.

5. Except for spouses, the property being disclaimed must go to someone other than the disclaimant—we know, we know, it's redundant!
6. The disclaimant cannot direct who the property will pass to and cannot have control over the property.
7. The disclaimer must comply with state law.

By disclaiming an IRA, the disclaimant also avoids the income tax obligation that would be due when distributions were made from the IRA. The taxation due is shifted to whomever received the IRA as a result of the disclaimer. Plans and custodians do not have to accept the disclaimer.

DON'T TRIP UP!

If the assets are in a qualified plan, make sure to comply with the state law where the deceased lived, but also the state law where the retirement plan was administered.

Why Disclaim?

1. An older beneficiary of an IRA disclaims so that a younger beneficiary can stretch the IRA over a longer period of time. To illustrate: Grandpa dies and has listed his son, Bob, as primary beneficiary of his IRA. Granddaughter Allison is named as contingent beneficiary. Bob does not need the money, so he disclaims his interest in the IRA, and it then passes to his daughter Allison, who then becomes the designated beneficiary. Allison uses her life expectancy to take required minimum distributions from grandpa's IRA. Allison is a non-spouse beneficiary, so she must remain as the beneficiary of the IRA; she cannot rollover grandpa's IRA into her own.

2. If the IRA owner mistakenly left his trust listed as his IRA beneficiary rather than his spouse, as he had intended. A disclaimer may be able to fix the mistake. To illustrate: The IRA owner names a trust as beneficiary and his spouse is the trustee of the trust. When the IRA owner dies, the spouse can disclaim the benefits of the IRA as trustee of the trust. The benefits then pass to the spouse as contingent beneficiary, rather than the trust. Spouse can then rollover the IRA to her own or remain as beneficiary of the inherited IRA.

Another illustration: IRA owner named his estate as beneficiary or had no beneficiary listed, instead of his spouse as he intended. If the spouse is the residual beneficiary under the IRA owner's will, a disclaimer might still get the benefits to the spouse.

Things to Remember With Disclaimers:

- Disclaiming is not always a slam-dunk process. Before you disclaim, it is important to seek qualified legal advice.

- Partial disclaimers can be made, but they are more complex. Be sure to hire a knowledgeable attorney when anticipating the use of a disclaimer, and review IRS regulation 25.2518-3.

- Don't designate specific names in a disclaimer. Doing so may be interpreted as a disclaimant trying to direct where the property will go.

- Don't take any distributions from an IRA unless necessary for a required minimum distribution the deceased did not take in the year of death. If a RMD must be taken, submit a statement to the custodian that the beneficiary is not accepting the entire IRA, just the RMD. Revenue Ruling 2005-36 specifically allows for the distribution of the RMD for the deceased IRA owner in the year of death. In other words, it's not considered acceptance of the IRA.

- Don't make any investment changes inside the IRA.

- Do your homework on the state requirements for a qualified disclaimer to eliminate last minute problems.

- Make sure the beneficiaries have clear guidance as to their choices after the IRA owner has died, and the ramifications of disclaiming.

Life Insurance

There are several uses and strategies for life insurance relating to a comprehensive financial and estate plan. We will focus on the four that we believe can benefit the most people in today's current economic environment.

The most popular use of life insurance is to protect families from the terrible financial consequences that can occur when a loved one passes away. Life insurance gives families a chance to mourn and to move on with their lives, providing them with choices that allow them time to heal.

There are two basic forms of life insurance: term and permanent. Let's examine them individually.

Term insurance provides coverage for a specified term of years in exchange for a specified premium. The policy does not accumulate cash value. There are three key factors to be considered in term insurance:

1. Face amount (death benefit)
2. Premium to be paid (cost of insurance)
3. The term (years of coverage)

The face amount of the policy can remain constant or decline. The premium can remain level or increase. The longer the term (or level period of the face amount of the policy), the more the premium will cost. The term can be for one or more years and the premium can remain level for that set number of years, whether it's 10, 20 or 30. After the level period is over, the premium will go up and continue going up as you grow older.

One of the most important questions you should ask before purchasing term insurance (or permanent insurance, which we'll get to shortly) is, "How long do I want to keep it?" If your answer is 10 or 20 years then a 10 or 20-year level term policy may be best for you. If your answer is something like, "Forever," or "Until I die," then you may want to consider a policy that will last as long as you do.

This brings us to *permanent insurance*, which falls under the categories of whole life, universal life, variable life and indexed universal life. Permanent insurance usually remains in force until the policy matures in the form of a death benefit (assuming it is funded properly with the correct premiums and the premiums are paid.) It builds cash value that you the policy owner can access by withdrawing money, borrowing the cash value, or surrendering the policy and receiving the surrender value. Proceeds paid by the insurer upon death of the insured are not included in gross income for federal and state income tax purposes, but if the proceeds are included in the estate of the deceased, it is likely they will be subject to federal and state estate tax.

Often the best solution is to have some term insurance to cover temporary needs and goals such as college funding and mortgage protection plus some permanent insurance to cover longer-term needs and additional goals such as wealth transfer, estate planning, charitable giving or simply giving your children and grandchildren a head start. The combination of the two provides you with control, options and flexibility in your overall financial plan. Additionally, there are temporary goals

A second use of permanent insurance, one that is especially important in today's economic environment, is *using the cash value accumulation inside permanent life insurance as a retirement supplement.* Today's turbulent economy has created so much uncertainty about the financial state of the government, massive deficits, continued spending, the solvency of Social Security and state pensions. These concerns come on top of worries about the viability of Medicare, a program that seems to be heading toward disaster as the largest demographic population (baby boomers) moves into retirement and will demand its share of entitlement benefits. Because of this, some people (as we noted in Chapter 1) are now starting to question the long-cherished belief they that they will be in a lower tax bracket when they retire—which will mean that they won't need as much money to live on. But given that tax rates today are the lowest they've been in decades and can only go up, if you no longer believe that argument or may be in a higher bracket, then you may want to position some of your money in asset classes or investment vehicles that do *not* ring the cash registers of the federal government. Two popular tools for doing that are the Roth IRA (see Chapter 6) and life insurance since both will allow you to access all the cash tax-free if structured properly. This is a proactive rather than a reactive retirement and tax planning strategy that places you no longer at the mercy of whatever the federal government decides to tax you when you retire.

Yet another strategy, if implemented properly, may turn out to make the purchase of permanent life insurance one of the best decisions you have ever made. Let's assume you are in retirement and have a two million dollar portfolio that you are counting on to provide income for you and your spouse for the rest of your lives. If you are like most retirees in this country you will live off your interest, dividends, pension, and Social Security and not touch your principal—because one thing most retirees have in common is that they do not like to spend principal for fear of running out of money.

FROM THE HORSE'S MOUTH

Life insurance can be a powerful retirement supplement, especially if funded properly since money can be accessed tax-free. So if you believe that based on the current tax rates you may be in a higher tax bracket down the road then this can be a very attractive retirement supplement. Remember, many of these tax deductions, like mortgages, children and 401K contributions may not be available to reduce your income when you retire.

And so, in the 1980's and 90's, advisors like us used to recommend to our clients taking a distribution of 7% a year out of their portfolios during retirement. We felt that percentage was a safe amount to withdraw without fear of running out of money. That percentage worked well in the good old days when markets went up every year by 10 to 20 percent. But the past decade has been a wake-up call that markets unfortunately go down as well—*sometimes way down.*

As a result, most advisors have now revised their recommended distribution rate to a more conservative 3 to 4% per year. Now, if you have a two million dollar portfolio, a 4% distribution rate amounts to $80,000 a year. Well, suppose after you elect to go with that rate, you find out that your deceased father has left you a two million dollar inheritance. Would knowing this in advance affect the way you decide to deplete your current retirement account? Of course it would. If you knew for sure that your own two million dollar retirement account would be replenished by a two million dollar inheritance, you could take withdrawals from principal at a 7% (or higher) distribution rate, giving you and your spouse an 80% *increase* in income a year if you amortized the two million principal over 20 years.

Of course, like most of us you may not have a dad who can leave you a two million dollar inheritance. But the good news is that you can have the next best thing. A permanent life insurance policy would allow you to spend down your principal while still protecting your spouse if you pass away by replacing those assets with a different form of inheritance—life insurance—and all of it tax-free! And if you live beyond those 20 years and deplete your principal you also have a backup plan in place: the cash value of your life insurance policy. If you design this strategy properly you can potentially have more income during retirement and leave more money to your family tax-free. Remember, we said it could be one of the best decisions you have ever made. And we're right!

Life insurance is also widely accepted as a very efficient vehicle for transferring wealth from one generation to another. Wealth transfer planning can be as simple as leaving a legacy to a loved one or a more sophisticated strategy for paying estate taxes the federal government imposes on those who are more affluent so that your heirs don't have to.

The idea of transferring money to those we love is a "want" issue rather than a "need" issue. In today's world it's all about what we keep and not what we make. By paying a small premium upfront for life insurance there can be a much larger reward later on—an explosion of wealth for your loved ones when that policy matures upon your death. Where else can you get such a large return on your investment that is all tax-free? This is one of the biggest benefits in the tax code and should not be ignored.

FROM THE HORSE'S MOUTH

"The single best, most cost-effective yet amazingly underutilized strategy for protecting retirement account balances, especially large ones, from being decimated by the highest levels of combined taxation is buying life insurance to offset the tax burden beneficiaries may face."

– Ed Slott, The Retirement Savings Time Bomb

A "need" issue involved with wealth transfer, especially for the affluent, would be this: As a person's wealth grows in this country, silent liens called estate taxes are placed upon it by the government. When that wealth gets above an applicable federal estate tax exemption (currently $5 million), it becomes subject to approximately 35 percent taxation of all assets *above that exemption amount*. This is on top of whatever the state estate tax may be in your individual state. These taxes would be due within nine months from the date of your death. Now, if you are like a lot of wealthy Americans, your estate may be comprised of real estate, business assets and IRAs. All are very illiquid assets, which means that if your heirs need to turn them into cash to pay ordinary income or capital gains taxes, the result may be a huge bite out your estate—on top of whatever losses that may result if the fair market value of those assets are depressed when liquidated.

Life insurance is often the best solution to counteract this. Instead of paying estate taxes by liquidating estate assets, you can just pay the much smaller insurance premium to invest in a life insurance policy and let the life insurance pay all the taxes! In the case of larger IRAs, you can take a *double-taxed* asset and turn it into a *double tax-free* asset: life insurance! By doing so, that which you have worked your entire life to accumulate can be kept intact for those you love.

FROM THE HORSE'S MOUTH

Permanent insurance can now also include coverage to pay for long-term care costs. Often times you can get needed life insurance and also provide a pool of money to pay for long term care at the same time. In today's uncertain economy, it is so important to make smart choices with your money and have one dollar accomplish the work of several dollars.

Life insurance offers the most efficient method of leveraging your assets. Every life insurance payment will reduce the size of your estate—the money is gone and the insurance is owned outside of your estate.

Be certain that *you* do not own the life insurance policy. In other words, you do not want it in your estate. *Instead, make sure your beneficiaries or a trust own the insurance.* The policy and the benefits it will pay will therefore be excluded from your estate. The proceeds then become available to pay the estate tax, so the IRA does not have to be invaded. This leaves your beneficiaries with the ability to stretch 100% of the IRA over decades. If you happen to use most of your IRA while you are alive, good for you! It was your money, anyway. The insurance can act as an IRA alternative, providing tax-free money as the inheritance.

To assure you that we don't speak with "forked tongue," we will confess that we, personally, own a tremendous amount of life insurance. The tax code allows life insurance benefits to be paid not only income tax free but also estate tax free through proper ownership as described. This is one of the last big benefits in the tax code and should not be ignored—it's your loss if you do.

Trying to determine how much insurance to own is a different story, because you have to project the worth of your estate before you die, which is impossible to do. Buy enough while you are young—at least enough to cover 40-50% of what you think your estate will be worth. Since we also don't know when we will die, we have another moving target to deal with. My personal suggestion: buy what you think you will need now while you are healthy, because insurance is always cheaper today than it will be tomorrow.

An alternative type of life insurance is a second-to-die, or survivorship, policy. This is often cheaper to buy than a single life policy because it insures the lives of the husband and wife together, and pays benefits only at the death of the second spouse. It is frequently used when one spouse is uninsurable, or a single life policy would be prohibitively expensive.

> ### FROM THE HORSE'S MOUTH
>
> *"Life insurance is one of the last great tax shelters left and a powerful countermeasure to the prevailing strategy of seeking less income in retirement due to being in a lower tax bracket. That may have been true once, but not anymore. Tax brackets are lower today than they've been in fifty years. The government needs money and taxes are going up. Life insurance is a great tax play for adding retirement income because there are no taxes on the internal cash value build-up at distribution—just like the Roth IRA."*
>
> – Dave Buckwald, Atlas Advisory Group

Long-Term Care Insurance

Also called extended care insurance, long-term care insurance is a type of insurance developed specifically to cover the costs of long-term care services in your home such as assistance with activities of daily living as well as care in a variety of facility and community settings, most of which are not covered by traditional health insurance or Medicare.

There is a great deal of choice and flexibility in long-term care insurance policies. You can select a range of care options and benefits that allow you to get the services you need in the settings that suit you best. With long-term care insurance, you pay premiums in amounts you know in advance and can budget for, and the policy pays—up to its coverage limits—for the long-term care you need when you need it.

"Long-term care insurance has *nothing* to do with the person who purchases the policy," explains Harley Gordon, founder of the National Academy of Elder Law Attorneys, author of *In Sickness and In Health* (Financial Strategies Press, 2007), and a leading authority on elder law issues. "Most people—including the media and even those who sell it—believe the policy protects the buyer. Not true. It enables the buyer to keep their financial commitments to their loved ones in the event of a protracted—and costly—medical care issue. Since the policy allows for money earmarked to go for that care, their portfolio remains intact, and all aspects of their retirement and estate plan continue unabated."

Long-term care insurance is not for everyone, Gordon stipulates. "But it is for anyone who loves their family and understands how devastating the consequences could be without it," he says. "It's been statistically proven by numerous national health care studies that taking care of a chronically ill person for a period of time will make even a healthy caregiver become chronically ill too. It sucks the life out of the caregiver. And if the caregiver is the family unit, that unit doesn't grow closer together from the experience but typically falls apart. That's the physical and emotional cost.

"The financial cost is great too—because if you don't allocate *some* money in your retirement portfolio to purchase a policy to pay for your care, you'll wind up allocating *everything* in your portfolio. This is not a *risk* proposition. It's a *consequence* proposition. Long-term care insurance is all about consequences. In other words, how severe would the consequences be to those you love without it? Are the consequences acceptable? If not, how can you protect your family from those consequences? Failure to address these issues leads to confusion, frustration and strained relationships between family members who have no frame of reference for who is going to provide the care, where it is going to be provided or who will coordinate it. Simple as that."

So, where should you go to get the best advice on setting up an extended care plan for your retirement needs? "The best option is to contact your local Alzheimers, Parkinson's, Multiple Sclerosis, Association of Retarded Citizens or other non-profit support group in your region and ask for a list of elder law attorneys in your area," Harley Gordon says. "I can almost guarantee that the list of names each group provides will be practically identical. Why? Because these groups will *know* these people from working with them, and they'll know these people have truly earned the right to be called 'specialists," in planning and putting together an extended care plan for retirees in need."

FROM THE **Horse's Mouth**

Permanent insurance can now also include coverage to pay for extended care costs if needed through the use of a rider. Riders are modifications to the insurance policy added at the same time the policy is issued. These riders change the basic policy to provide some feature desired by the policy owner.

The Irrevocable Life Insurance Trust

The **Irrevocable Life Insurance Trust** (ILIT) is a trust designed to own *permanent* life insurance, which is not subject to amendment or termination at the whim of the creator of the trust or its beneficiaries. Usually, the ILIT owns insurance on the life of its creator but can also insure the creator's spouse. Upon the death of the insured person(s), the proceeds of the insurance are paid into the trust. The goal of such a trust is to shift the ownership of the policies from the insured's generation to a younger generation, in order to remove the policy proceeds from taxation at the death of the insured and/or spouse. The family can have a fund of cash used to create liquidity in an estate for payment of estate taxes without having to liquidate any assets.

When the insurance proceeds are paid into the trust following the death of the insured, there is no tax due on the payment, assuming all the legal requirements for the trust have been fulfilled. No estate tax and no income tax are due on the entire insurance policy proceeds. The assets in the trust are then distributed to the named beneficiaries according to the terms of the trust as to individual beneficiary, timing of distributions and amounts.

HORSE SENSE

A trustee is named to handle the operation of the trust, in accordance with the provisions of the trust both prior to the death of the insured and following the receipt of the insurance proceeds. The trustee is normally an individual or an institution selected by the insured to act independently of the insured since exercise and control by the insured could reverse the tax advantages of the trust and open the trust to creditors. For example, you can choose an institutional trustee to act on behalf of your children should something happen to you and your wife. The selection of a trustee is critical to the success of the trust—especially in the context of the insured's goals. The trustee will oversee investments, distributions, etc. The permanency of the trust also underscores the importance of trustee selection.

The insurance proceeds are not included in the insured's estate or subject to estate tax on the death of the insured. If the trust takes advantage of the annual gift tax exclusion, then transfer tax on the premiums will also be avoided. It is possible that the ILIT can make distributions to grandchildren and other future generations without there being liability for the Generation Skipping Transfer Tax.

In the trust document, the creator of the trust has the ability to provide for the ultimate disposition of the insurance proceeds. Rather than giving the funds of the trust to beneficiaries in a lump sum, the trust may provide for certain conditions before distributions may be made. The beneficiaries may have to reach a certain age or educational level. A beneficiary may have to hold employment or complete a substance abuse program. The careful drafting of the terms for distribution permits a great deal of control and specificity on the part of the insured, providing a sense of confidence that the

> **FROM THE HORSE'S MOUTH** . . .
>
> *The ILIT is a very useful means of creating and protecting wealth. The purchase of the insurance will later generate wealth in the form of the insurance death benefit. Those proceeds, properly invested, may grow over time, adding to the wealth initially created through the insurance payout. When an ILIT is used in conjunction with other estate planning techniques, the insurance proceeds may be used to replace wealth that is transferred to non-family beneficiaries such as charitable beneficiaries. The existence of life insurance protects wealth by providing an alternative to the liquidation of assets at the death of the owner.*

inherited money is used in accordance with the insured's wishes.

The issue of the trust owning new or existing insurance on the life of the trust creator is beyond the scope of this book. Many estate planning practitioners prefer that the trust apply for and obtain new insurance on the life of the creator. In this case, the trust is formed prior to the application for insurance and should make the application through the trustee. This assumes the trust creator is insurable, which may not always be the case. If the creator of the trust is uninsurable or prefers to transfer existing insurance to the trust, the creator must survive for at least three years after the transfer by gifting existing insurance to the trust. If the insured dies within the three year period, the insurance proceeds are pulled back into the estate of the insured and taxed as part of the estate.

When existing insurance is transferred to a trust, the creator must properly value the policy at the time of transfer and assess the appropriate amount of tax due upon the gift of the policy. Gifts of insurance generally are valued for gift tax purposes at the "interpolated terminal reserve value," which is usually close to the cash surrender value for a reasonably healthy individual. The face value of the policy is often many times greater than this gift tax value. If the insured becomes temporarily uninsurable, or even just falls into poor health, the policy gifted may have a value exponentially greater than amount of gift tax due upon the transfer of the policy into the trust.

The most efficient method of paying the insurance premiums by the trust is to use the insured's **annual gifts** (gifts that qualify for the annual exclusion from gift tax under IRC Section 2503) of the premium amount, and apply the annual gift tax exclusion to the transfers. This approach requires annual notice to the trust beneficiaries of the gift to them of the amount intended to fund annual premiums. It also allows the beneficiaries the right to demand from the trustee that a portion of the total gift be attributable to their share in the trust. The beneficiaries decline to take their share of the transferred funds from the trust and those funds are used to pay the annual insurance premium on the trust-owned policy. The transfer qualifies for the annual tax exclusion as a current gift because of the beneficiary's ability to demand their share of the gift. This is called the **demand power** or **"Crummey" power**, which comes from the law suit Crummey v. Comm., 397F.2d 82(9th Cir. 1968).

This is but an overview of the ILIT. As with any estate planning document, you should hire an attorney who specializes in this field to help. Also consider consulting a financial advisor to help you crunch the numbers to determine the best approach for your family.

Income in Respect of a Decedent

Certain items do not receive a step up in basis at the owner's death. These are called **Income in Respect of a Decedent** (IRD) items. Since IRD assets do not receive the step up, the beneficiaries of IRD receive a carryover in basis which is the same basis as the decedent had prior to death. IRD is income earned by the decedent but is not realized until after death, so taxes haven't yet been paid. When the beneficiary inherits this income, it is time to pay taxes. The biggest IRD assets are retirement accounts and annuities. This puts retirement benefits and IRA money in the unfortunate position of being subject to both income and estate tax. The government, in its generosity, decided to give us a break and create an income tax deduction for beneficiaries subject to this double taxation—the IRD deduction.

The effect of the IRD deduction is to lower the beneficiary's tax bracket on the inherited IRA's distributions. This may make taking distributions from an inherited IRA more tax-efficient than taking them from a personal IRA. A distribution from the inherited IRA is also not subject to an early withdrawal penalty. Don't get too excited! Think of it this way: you just lost $20,000 on the Kentucky Derby but Churchill Downs wants to thank you for coming, and gives your wife a complimentary burger and mint julep after you leave the race track.

Not every beneficiary qualifies for the IRD deduction. A 1099-R Form must be generated for the beneficiary describing the distribution.

Step 1. Look at box 7 on the form. If the number 4 is printed in box 7, the distribution was made to a beneficiary.

Step 2. Federal estate tax must have been paid on the IRA you inherited. If no federal estate tax was paid, there is no IRD deduction. If federal estate tax was paid, then you qualify for the deduction.

Remember that the deduction goes to the beneficiary who received the taxable distribution from the inherited IRA regardless of whether she is the one actually paying the estate tax.

Calculating the deduction is beyond the scope of this book. We recommend you hire a CPA to calculate the deduction. Trust us, it will be worth every penny—because it could mean thousands of dollars on larger estates. The key is to understand that the deduction exists and how to spot it.

NOTES

CHAPTER 8

YOUR RETIREMENT PLAN CHECKLIST

As we've noted throughout this book, it's important to educate yourself on all aspects of retirement distribution planning so that you will know what questions to ask your financial and legal advisors when creating your plan. Now that you have read our book, you're well equipped to ask those questions.

Use the following checklist to be sure you and your advisors have covered all the key points of income, tax, asset, and risk planning in creating your plan. Check "yes" for each item you have attended to. For items that you have not yet taken into account, check off "no," and use the blank spaces after that item to make a note to bring this up with your advisor. Nothing should be overlooked or forgotten. Remember, it's YOUR money. So, whether you choose to retire a winner or not, it's all up to you.

1)   I have taken into consideration inflation and have been conservative in my planning, using a 3 to 4% per year inflation rate.

[   ] YES   [   ] NO

_____

_____

2)   I have assumed a life expectancy beyond normal life expectancy in my retirement plan.

[   ] YES [   ] NO

_____

_____

3)   I have thought about the amount of money I want to leave behind for my heirs in my retirement plan and my spending budget is set to allow for that.

[   ] YES [   ] NO

_____

_____

4)   I have taken into consideration what is important to my family and me and my retirement plan is built around those things.

[   ] YES [   ] NO

_____

_____

5)   I have thought about additional budget items during my retirement such as new cars, housing expenses, dental, medical, grandchildren's college, etc.

[   ] YES [   ] NO

_____

_____

6) My retirement plan allows me to see my progress toward my long-term goals and measure my path to success.

[   ] YES [   ] NO

---

7) My retirement plan allows me to know how market changes will affect my ability to maintain my retirement goals.

[   ] YES [   ] NO

---

8) My retirement plan takes into consideration the possibility of higher taxes.

[   ] YES [   ] NO

---

9) My retirement plan is based on net numbers so it can easily be adjusted for changes in the tax code.

[   ] YES [   ] NO

---

10) My retirement plan has been stress-tested to take into consideration the possibility of poor market conditions at any point in my retirement.

[   ] YES [   ] NO

---

11) My retirement plan has been stress-tested to take into consideration the possibility of a pre-mature death and the effects on the surviving spouse.

[   ] YES [   ] NO

12) My retirement plan has been stress-tested to determine the impact of a long-term care expense versus the cost of long term care insurance to make sure my money is used most efficiently.

[   ] YES [   ] NO

13) I have included in my retirement plan the possibility of using life insurance instead of long-term care insurance since mortality is 100% and there is no way to determine if long-term care expenses will be incurred.

[   ] YES [   ] NO

14) My retirement plan is built to allow me to have the highest possibility of achieving my goals and do so with the least amount of risk possible.

[   ] YES [   ] NO

15) My retirement plan takes into consideration the effects of taking Social Security early and the long-term impact of not only how much I will receive from Social Security but how it effects my ability to meet my long-term goals.

[   ] YES [   ] NO

16) My retirement plan takes into consideration the possibility that Social Security can be taken tax-free even with spendable income of more than $50,000 per year.

[   ] YES [   ] NO

17) My retirement plan considers taxes in such a way that I will know which account to spend from first to keep taxes as low as possible.

[   ] YES [   ] NO

18) My retirement plan includes calculations to determine when my spouse should start taking Social Security and if he/she could take the spousal benefit first and defer to 70½ to maximize the benefit.

[   ] YES [   ] NO

19) My retirement plan can alert me if I have gotten off track so that my advisor can give me suggestions for getting back on track.

[   ] YES [   ] NO

20) Most of my retirement plan is tailored specifically to my family's long- and short term goals and the question "what could possibly go wrong?" has been asked in all areas, with contingencies in place to mitigate the risk of not achieving those goals.

[   ] YES [   ] NO

21) During my accumulation years I built up money in taxable, tax deferred and tax-free accounts in the proper amounts in order to keep my taxes flexible in my distribution (retirement) years.

[ ] YES [   ] NO

22) I have conducted a Roth Conversion analysis by first completing my comprehensive retirement income strategy then overlaying the results of the Roth conversion to determine the appropriate (if any) amount of my traditional IRA to convert to a Roth.

[ ] YES [   ] NO

23) I have considered the effects of NUA on my 401(k) distribution and how it may or may not reduce future income tax.

[ ] YES [   ] NO

24) My current retirement plan is forward-looking and utilizes today's tax laws to attempt to minimize taxes in the coming years.

[ ] YES [   ] NO

25) I have based my retirement plan on the assumption that taxes will be higher in the future and I have taken all the steps necessary to help mitigate the effects of higher taxes.

[ ] YES [   ] NO

26) I have a pro-active retirement planning advisor and CPA who work together to help lower my current taxes and in years looking forward.

[   ] YES [   ] NO

---

27) I have been through an exercise that allows me to see the best way to spend my assets during retirement.

[   ] YES [   ] NO

---

28) I have tested my plan to see if Municipal Bonds could be of value.

[   ] YES [   ] NO

---

29) I understand that Social Security income is tax-free unless I disqualify myself.

[   ] YES [   ] NO

---

30) My retirement plan has included looking at annuities to see if their tax benefits would work in my situation.

[   ] YES [   ] NO

NOTES

APPENDIX A

RMD Worksheet, Transfer Tax Exemptions, Uniform Distribution Table, Single Life Expectancy Table

(Keep for Your Records)

1. Age	70½	71½	72½	73½	74½
2. Year age was reached					
3. Value of IRA at the close of business on December 31 of the year immediately prior to the year on line 2[1]					
4. Distribution period from Table III or life expectancy from Life Expectancy Table I or Table II[2]					
5. Required distribution (divide line 3 by 4)[3]					
1. Age	75½	76½	77½	78½	79½
2. Year age was reached					
3. Value of IRA at the close of business on December 31 of the year immediately prior to the year on line 2[1]					
4. Distribution period from Table III or life expectancy from Life Expectancy Table I or Table II[2]					
5. Required distribution (divide line 3 by 4)[3]					
1. Age	80½	81½	82½	83½	84½
2. Year age was reached					
3. Value of IRA at the close of business on December 31 of the year immediately prior to the year on line 2[1]					
4. Distribution period from Table III or life expectancy from Life Expectancy Table I or Table II[2]					
5. Required distribution (divide line 3 by 4)[3]					
1. Age	85½	86½	87½	88½	89½
2. Year age was reached					
3. Value of IRA at the close of business on December 31 of the year immediately prior to the year on line 2[1]					
4. Distribution period from Table III or life expectancy from Life Expectancy Table I or Table II[2]					
5. Required distribution (divide line 3 by 4)[3]					

[1] If you have more than one IRA, you must figure the required distribution separately for each IRA.

[2] Use the appropriate life expectancy or distribution period for each year and for each IRA.

[3] If you have more than one IRA, you must withdraw an amount equal to the total of the required distributions figured for each IRA. You can, however, withdraw the total from one IRA or from more than one IRA.

Current Federal Estate Tax and Generation Skipping
Transfer Tax Exemptions

(If history is any guide, the one thing you can be sure of is that the federal estate tax exemption is constantly changing—as shown in this snapshot of the years 2001 to 2011.)

Year	Estate Tax Exemption	Top Estate Tax (& GST Tax) Rate
2001	$675,000	55% (prior law)
2002	$1,000,000	50%
2003	$1,000,000	49%
2004	$1,500,000	48%
2005	$1,500,000	47%
2006	$2,000,000	46%
2007	$2,000,000	45%
2008	$2,000,000	45%
2009	$3,500,000	45%
2010	Estate Tax is Repealed	-0-%
2011	$5,000,000	35%
GST Exemption Amounts:		
2001	$1,060,000	
2002	$1,100,000	
2003	$1,120,000	
2004	$1,500,000	
2005	$1,500,000	
2006	$2,000,000	
2007	$2,000,000	
2008	$2,000,000	
2009	$3,500,000	
2010	GST is repealed	
2011	$2,000,000 (indexed for inflation)	

Uniform Distribution Table

This table is the new life expectancy table to be used by IRA owners to calculate lifetime distributions (unless your beneficiary is your spouse who is more than 10 years younger than you). In that case, you would not use this table, you would use the actual joint life expectancy of you and your spouse based on the regular joint live expectancy table. The Uniform Distribution Table is never used by IRA beneficiaries to compute required distributions on their inherited IRAs.

Age of IRA Owner or Plan Participant	Life Expectancy (in years)	Age of IRA Owner or Plan Participant	Life Expectancy (in years)
70	27.4	93	9.6
71	26.5	94	9.1
72	25.6	95	8.6
73	24.7	96	8.1
74	23.8	97	7.6
75	22.9	98	7.1
76	22.0	99	6.7
77	21.2	100	6.3
78	20.3	101	5.9
79	19.5	102	5.5
80	18.7	103	5.2
81	17.9	104	4.9
82	17.1	105	4.5
83	16.3	106	4.2
84	15.5	107	3.9
85	14.8	108	3.7
86	14.1	109	3.4
87	13.4	110	3.1
88	12.7	111	2.9
89	12.0	112	2.6
90	11.4	113	2.4
91	10.8	114	2.1
92	10.2	115 and older	1.9

Single Life Expectancy Table for Inherited IRAs

(to be used for calculated post-death required distributions to beneficiaries)

Designated beneficiaries use this single life expectancy table based on their age in the year after the IRA owner's death. That factor is reduced by one for each succeeding distribution year. Spouse beneficiaries who do not elect to roll the IRA over or treat it as their own, also use the single life table, but they can recalculate each year.

0	82.4	28	55.3	56	28.7	84	8.1
1	81.6	29	54.3	57	27.9	85	7.6
2	80.6	30	53.3	58	27.0	86	7.1
3	79.7	31	52.4	59	26.1	87	6.7
4	78.7	32	51.4	60	25.2	88	6.3
5	77.7	33	50.4	61	24.4	89	5.9
6	76.7	34	49.4	62	23.5	90	5.5
7	75.8	35	48.5	63	22.7	91	5.2
8	74.8	36	47.5	64	21.8	92	4.9
9	73.8	37	46.5	65	21.0	93	4.6
10	72.8	38	45.6	66	20.2	94	4.3
11	71.8	39	44.6	67	19.4	95	4.1
12	70.8	40	43.6	68	18.6	96	3.8
13	69.9	41	42.7	69	17.8	97	3.6
14	68.9	42	41.7	70	17.0	98	3.4
15	67.9	43	40.7	71	16.3	99	3.1
16	66.9	44	39.8	72	15.5	100	2.9
17	66.0	45	38.8	73	14.8	101	2.7
18	65.0	46	37.9	74	14.1	102	2.5
19	64.0	47	37.0	75	13.4	103	2.3
20	63.0	48	36.0	76	12.7	104	2.1
21	62.1	49	35.1	77	12.1	105	1.9
22	61.1	50	34.2	78	11.4	106	1.7
23	60.1	51	33.3	79	10.8	107	1.5
24	59.1	52	32.3	80	10.2	108	1.4
25	58.2	53	31.4	81	9.7	109	1.2
26	57.2	54	30.5	82	9.1	110	1.1
27	56.2	55	29.6	83	8.6	111+	1.0

APPENDIX B
DIVORCE, RETIREMENT PLANS AND IRAS

Even in the midst of what might be a very difficult divorce, you need to make informed financial decisions regarding the division of the property you and your spouse have accumulated during your marriage. Retirement savings are one of the largest assets many people own and therefore, become an important issue in divorce proceedings. If you are separated or divorced and a spouse has an employer-sponsored retirement plan such as a 401(k) or pension plan, each party may be legally entitled to a portion of those benefits. How can an interest in a retirement plan be protected? Consider using a QDRO.

Qualified Domestic Relations Order

A Qualified Domestic Relations Order (QDRO) creates or recognizes the existence of an alternative payee's right to receive benefits payable under a pension plan. Certain information must be provided, and clear requirements must be met (see: ERISA 206(d)(3)(B)(i); IRC 414(p)(1)(A)). However, a QDRO may also assign an alternative payee the right to receive all, or a portion, of the benefits. An alternative payee cannot be anyone other than a spouse, former spouse, child, or other dependent of a participant (see: ERISA 206(d)(3)(K); IRC 414(p)(8)).

Would you like this in simpler English? A QDRO is a special kind of court order which is used to divide pension rights between divorcing spouses, or to collect alimony or child support from an employee benefit plan. These plans include 401(k), 403(b), 457, defined benefit monthly payments, TIAA/CREF, etc. A QDRO will avoid negative tax implications due to the splitting of the retirement benefits. The person whose interest is being transferred is the "participant," while the person receiving benefits is the "alternate payee."

A QDRO can assign rights to pension benefits under more than one pension plan of the same or different employers as long as each plan and the assignment of benefit rights under each plan are clearly specified (see: ERISA 206(d)(3)(C)(iv); IRC 414(p)(2)(D)).

The reason to have a QDRO to access a share of the marital retirement assets is due to IRS regulations—a QDRO grants tax benefits to the employee or employer who contributed the benefit proceeds. The IRS does not permit anyone, not even a judge, to divide or transfer these assets unless and until the parties obtain a QDRO which complies with the Internal Revenue Code.

> ## FROM THE HORSE'S MOUTH
>
> *The QDRO can protect the receiver's distribution and not have to rely upon the ex-spouse to enact the distribution. Through a QDRO the Plan Administrator will implement the distribution. A QDRO cannot require the Plan to provide any form of benefit not otherwise provided under the Plan, nor allow increased benefits not otherwise allowed in the Plan. A QDRO can be quite complicated and if not drafted by a specialist, certain important and valuable information may not be addressed.*

The State divorce court first enters an order dividing a pension. This court order may be entered after a contested hearing or by mutual agreement of the parties. The order may be approved by the pension plan as a draft to save you court costs and attorney's fees, but your rights are not protected. You will not receive anything under the State court until the final order has been signed by a judge and accepted by the plan. The plan will want to see language written in a way that conforms to their administrative protocol. Even if the QDRO permits a former spouse to roll over an interest in a retirement plan, some plans will not permit it. Some plans will not make any distribution at all until you have reached a certain retirement age specified in the plan. Plan rules ultimately govern distributions, leaving the plan participant and the former spouse with little control over how they receive QDRO payments. If the plan allows for rollovers due to QDROs, the order will permit the account manager to carve the account into two pieces, one for each spouse. The portion that is rolled over to the former spouse belongs to the former spouse, and the required distribution rules apply as though the former spouse were the original owner.

These rules apply only to qualified plans if there is a QDRO in place. If there is no QDRO, the participant's retirement plan is treated as though it is entirely his/hers for required distribution purposes. If the divorce agreement states that the former spouse is to share in the retirement plan, the participant must generally give the former spouse his/her share as it is distributed from the plan. A portion of each distribution would go to the former spouse.

QDROs are not technically required for IRAs, but it may still be prudent to draft one. Certain changes in the tax law have permitted divorcing parties to transfer a portion of their IRA from one spouse to the other pursuant to a standard divorce decree or property settlement agreement. While the law may permit this, many banks, brokerage firms and IRA custodians are ill equipped to handle the transfer properly. The IRA custodian will gladly do the transfer, but it may create a taxable event for one or both parties because of the automatic reporting systems that most banks and brokerage firms use which notify the IRS of distributions and transfers into and out of IRA accounts. With a QDRO on file with the court, either or both parties can insist that the IRA custodian amend any incorrect IRS reports.

If some or all of an IRA is transferred into a former spouse's name as a result of a written divorce or separation agreement, the transferred portion belongs to the former spouse in every respect. The required minimum distribution rules apply as though the former spouse were the original owner.

This is a highly technical field and QDROs should be drafted by attorneys who specialize in divorce matters.

Distribution after Divorce

Let's look at an example of distribution after divorce: Norman and Norma Cohen divorced in 1997. Their financial matters were determined in a Court Order issued in 1999. Norman owned an IRA worth $120,000, half of which was to be transferred to Norma. Norma opened an IRA account and $60,000 was transferred from Norman's account.

Norma took a full withdrawal from the IRA but did not report the distribution on her income tax return. The IRS didn't appreciate that, and Norma wound up in Tax Court. Norma claimed she did not receive a 1099R, which proved she was aware that she took a distribution from the IRA and should have reported such on her Form 1040. With no income reported, the Tax Court sited Sec. 6662, which applies to the 20% substantial understatement penalty. Norma was issued a penalty of $4,450 in addition to the tax bill. Norma was also given the 10% early withdrawal penalty because she took the distribution before she reached age 59½. The triple whammy!

There is a difference in how IRAs and qualified plans are treated in divorce situations. Qualified plans are subject to QDROs. Payments under a QDRO are exempt from the 10% early withdrawal penalty tax. IRAs are not subject to QDROs but are governed by Code Sec. 408(d)(6). This states that the part of the IRA which is transferred to an ex-spouse under a settlement or Court Order is not treated as a taxable distribution. After the transfer is complete, the recipient is the owner of the IRA with all IRA rules applicable including the 10% early withdrawal penalty.

In Bougas v. Commissioner, T.C. Memo 2003-194, the Tax Court held that, when there is no QDRO and no "substantial compliance" with the requirements for a QDRO, the use of an IRA to satisfy payments required to an ex-wife under a divorce decree, even on the advice of counsel, was a premature distribution resulting in a 10% penalty under section 72(t).

> ## FROM THE HORSE'S MOUTH
>
> *Once the QDRO is enacted, the receiver may choose to take a one-time distribution allowed via 72(t) regulations. This non-penalized payment must occur prior to the funds' being distributed to the receiver's IRA. Distributions made in this manner may not be subject to the 10% penalty, but will be subject to income tax. Keep in mind that prior to the distribution the Plan Administrator must withhold 20% in taxes. For example if the receiver wishes to have $100,000 transferred, he/she must request $120,000 for the Plan Administrator.*

Mr. Bougas was ordered to make payments to Mrs. Bougas but Mr. Bougas had no liquid assets with which to make the payments. So, he took a distribution from his IRA. Mr. Bougas not only had to pay income tax on the distribution but was also stuck with a 10% early withdrawal penalty because he was under 59½. He complained to the court that he was unaware of a QDRO, and, had he known, he would have requested his attorney comply to avoid the taxation of the distribution and the early withdrawal penalty. The court ruled against him, and affirmed the imposition of a 10% penalty under IRC section 72(t). They basically told Mr. Bougas that ignorance on his part (or on the part of his attorney) is not a valid legal defense.

A much better alternative for Mr. Bougas would have been to pay Mrs. Bougas through an award of part of his IRA under a divorce decree or separation agreement. The IRA award would not have been taxed to Mr. Bougas and he could have avoided the penalty. Mrs. Bougas would then have been able to take distributions through a series of substantially equal periodic payments, and would also have avoided the 10% early withdrawal penalty. Both parties would have come out ahead, with fewer headaches, and less unnecessary taxation.

The lesson here should be clear: be careful when the property being divided includes retirement assets.

GLOSSARY

Adjustable Gross Estate—An amount calculated for the purpose of determining the availability of certain tax benefits, and arrived at by reducing the gross estate by allowable debts, funeral expenses, as well as medical costs and administrative expenses.

Adjusted Gross Income (AGI)—Total taxable income reduced by certain expenses such as qualified plan or IRA contributions or alimony payments. (Note: Adjusted gross income does not take into account any itemized deductions.)

Administrator (executor/executrix)—An administrator is appointed by the court to settle an estate. An executor, on the other hand, is named by the estate owner in the will as the one to settle the estate. The administrator is always appointed by the court and the executor is always named in the will.

After-tax Contribution—A contribution to a retirement plan or IRA for which no deduction was taken on an income tax return.

After-tax Dollars—The amount of income left after all income taxes have been withheld or paid.

Amortization—The reduction of a debt through periodic payments of principal and interest.

Annual Exclusion—A gift tax exclusion that a donor is allowed each year for each donation, provided the gift is one of a present interest.

Applicable Credit Amount—A credit to which the estate of every individual is entitled which can be directly applied against the gift or estate tax.

Applicable Exclusion Amount—Equivalent value of an individual's property offset by the applicable credit amount (often referred to as the credit equivalent).

Basis—An amount treated as the purchase price or cost of an asset for purposes of determining the taxable gain or loss when the asset is sold.

Beneficiary—The person or entity to receive the benefits from insurance or from trust property, such as a retirement plan or IRA, usually after the insured or the owner of the property dies.

Bypass Trust—A testamentary trust designed to keep property transferred to it by the decedent-spouse out of the surviving spouse's gross estate.

Charitable Deduction—A deduction allowed against a reportable gift to a charitable organization or as a deduction from the adjusted gross estate.

Charitable Remainder Trust—A trust that provides a remainder to one or more qualified charities.

Completed Transfer—A gift that is beyond the donor's recall.

Contingent Beneficiary—A person or entity who is entitled to receive the benefits of a retirement plan or IRA only if and when a specific event occurs, such as the death of a primary beneficiary.

Credit Shelter—The dollar level of assets that are protected by the estate exemption at death.

Crummey Powers—Rights granted to the beneficiaries of an irrevocable trust to demand all or a portion of a grantor's contribution to the trust, thereby creating a present interest in the grantor's gift.

Custodian—A person or entity who is in possession of property belonging to another. The custodian of an IRA is the institution that holds the account even though the property belongs to the individual who established and funded the account.

Deductible Contribution—A contribution or a retirement plan that an employer may claim as a business expense to offset income on the employer's tax return. You may know it as simply the employer's contribution. In the case of an IRA, a deductible contribution is one that an individual taxpayer may use to offset income on the individual's tax return.

Deferral Period—The number of years over which distributions from a retirement plan or IRA can be spread.

De Minimus Rule—Doctrine that the law does not concern itself with very small, unimportant matters.

Disclaimer—A renunciation of or a refusal to accept property to which a person is entitled by gift, by law, or under the terms of a will or a trust.

Distribution—A payout of property or cash from a retirement plan or IRA to the participant or a beneficiary.

Donor—The person who makes a gift. The term also refers to the person who grants a power of appointment to another.

Earned Income—Income received for providing goods or services. Earned income might be wages or salary, or net profit from a business.

Eligible Employee—An employee who has met certain conditions of an employer's retirement plan (such as years of service) and now qualifies to participate in the plan.

Estate—All the property an individual owns.

Estate Administration Expense—Expenses incurred in the collection and preservation of probate assets, the payment of estate debts, and the distribution of probate assets to estate beneficiaries.

Estate and Gift Tax Systems—Tax systems in which a tax burden is imposed on transfers made during life and at death.

Estate Tax—A tax imposed upon the right of a person to transfer property at death. This type of tax is imposed not only by the federal government, but also by a number of states.

Fair Market Value—The price at which an item could be sold at retail by a willing seller to a willing buyer.

Federal Estate Tax—An excise tax levied on the right to transfer property at death, imposed upon and measured by the value of the taxable estate left by the decedent.

Fiduciary—One occupying a legally defined position of trust.

Fiduciary Tax Return—The income tax return (Form 1041) filed by the fiduciary of an estate or a trust.

Future Interest—The postponed right of use or enjoyment of property.

Generation-Skipping Transfer—A taxable distribution or a taxable termination from a generation-skipping trust or its equivalent.

Gift (for tax purposes)—Property, property rights or interests gratuitously passed or transferred for less than an adequate and full consideration in money to another, in trust or directly or indirectly.

Gift Tax Marital Deduction—A deduction allowed for a gift made by one spouse to another.

Grantor—A person who creates a trust; also referred to as a settler, creator, or trustor.

Gross Estate—An amount determined by totaling the value of all the assets that the decedent had an interest in, which are required to be included in the estate by the Internal Revenue Code.

Heir—Technically, a person designated by law to succeed to the estate or an intestate, also known as next of kin.

Incidents of Ownership—Elements of ownership or degree of control over a life insurance policy.

Income in Respect of a Decedent (IRD)—Income that was earned by a cash-basis taxpayer but not actually or constructively received by the taxpayer's date of death.

Interpolated Terminal Reserve—The reserve on any life insurance policy between anniversary dates, regardless of whether future premium payments are due. It is determined by a pro rata adjustment upward (or downward in the case of certain term policies of long duration) between the previous terminal reserve and the next terminal reserve.

Inter Vivos Trust—A trust created during the settler's lifetime. It becomes operative during lifetime as opposed to a trust under will (testamentary trust), which does not become operative until the settler dies.

Irrevocable Trust—A trust that cannot be altered or terminated by the person who created it. Once assets are transferred to an irrevocable trust, the assets are subject to the terms of the trust for as long as the trust exists.

Itemized Deduction—Expenses, such as medical payments, mortgage interest, and charitable contributions that may be used to reduce AGI to arrive at the total amount of income subject to tax.

Lump Sum Distribution—A distribution or payment from a qualified employee benefit plan (which takes place in one taxable year to the recipient) of the entire account balance of an employee, which becomes payable to the recipient because of death, separation from service, or after age 59½.

Net Unrealized Appreciation—The amount by which an asset has appreciated in value before it is sold.

Nondeductible Contribution—A contribution to a retirement plan or IRA that may not be claimed as a business expense or used as an adjustment to offset taxable income on an income tax return.

Participant or Active Participant—An employee for whom the employer makes a contribution to the employer's retirement plan.

Per Capita Distribution—A method of dividing a decedent's estate according to the number of individuals inheriting the decedent's property, each individual sharing equally.

Per Stirpes Distribution—A method of dividing a decedent's estate by representation or family groups.

Present Interest—A present right to use or enjoy property.

Pre-tax Dollars—Total taxable income before the payment of income taxes.

Primary Beneficiary—A person or entity entitled to receive benefits from a retirement plan or IRA upon the death of the original participant.

Probate—The process of providing a will's validity in court, and executing its provisions under the guidance of the court. The process of probating the will involves recognition by the appropriate court of the executor named in the will (or appointment of an administrator if none has been named), and the determination of validity of the will if it is corrected.

Pro rata—Proportionately.

Prudent Person Rule—A rule stating that a fiduciary, in acquiring, investing, reinvesting, exchanging, retaining, selling, and managing property for the benefit of another, shall exercise the judgment and care under the circumstances then prevailing, that persons of prudence, discretion and intelligence exercise in the management of their own affairs.

Remainder Interest—A future interest that comes into existence after the termination of a prior interest.

Residuary Estate—The remaining part of a testator's estate, after payment of debts and bequests. Wills usually contain a clause or disposition of the residue of the estate that the testator has not otherwise bequeathed or devised.

Revocable Trust—A trust whose terms allow the creator of the trust to alter its provisions, cancel it, or remove some or all of the property from the trust and return the property to the creator.

Separation from Service—Official termination of employment.

Standard Deduction—A fixed dollar amount that may be used in place of itemized deductions to reduce AGI before computing tax liability.

Stepped-up Basis—The new basis acquired by a decedent's gross estate in which the decedent's property is increased to fair market value of the asset on the date of death.

Tax Bracket—The rate at which each additional dollar of income will be taxed.

Tax-Deductible Expenses—An item of expense that may be used to offset income on a tax return.

Traditional IRA—Any contributory or rollover IRA that is not a Roth IRA or a SIMPLE IRA.

Transfer Tax—Gift, estate or generation-skipping transfer tax on large transfers of property or money for less than adequate and full consideration.

Trustee—A person or entity who holds legal title to the property in a trust.

Vested Benefit—The portion of a participant's retirement plan accumulation that a participant may keep after leaving the employer who sponsors the plan; or the portion that goes to a participant's beneficiary if the participant dies.

Waiver—Intentional dismissal, as in the case of a penalty.

AUTHOR BIOGRAPHIES

DEAN BARBER, RFC

Dean Barber, founder and president of Barber Financial Group, began his career in the financial service industry on one of the bleakest days in recent history, October 19, 1987, Black Monday. It didn't take him long to realize that the answer doesn't lay in how much money a person makes; it's how much they keep. He has built one of Kansas City's premier financial management firms, specializing in assisting retirees, pre-retirees and business owners in building and preserving their wealth through the concepts of asset management, tax strategies and estate planning. Dean has become a nationally known authority on financial planning and advice. Since 2003, he has hosted a (now nationally) syndicated radio program, *America's Wealth Management Show*. He has been a regular contributor for many publications and broadcasts for news programs, such as the Wall Street Journal, *Fox Business News, CNBC, www.Bankrate.com*, the *International Business Times, U.S. News & World Report, Forbes, Small Business CEO Magazine, www.NewYorkTimes.com, www.InvestmentNews. com, BusinessWeek, www.Portfolio.com, Kansas City Business Journal, KMBC-9TV* and *KSHB-41TV*. His weekly radio program features guests like economist Harry Dent and Ed Slott, the CPA most often quoted by the *Wall Street Journal*. He has also lectured and presented to key employees for several Fortune 500 corporations. This is his first book.

MICHAEL E. BROWN, AIFA, CFP, CMA

Mike is a General Securities Principal, an Accredited Investment Fiduciary Auditor (AIFA) through the Center for Fiduciary Studies at the Katz Graduate School of Business, a Certified Financial Planner (CFP) through the College for Financial Planning, and a Certified Investment Management Analyst (CIMA) through the Wharton School at the University of Pennsylvania. He is the author of the book "The IRA Winners Circle: Expert Advice to Make Your IRA a Winner" and in 2005 Worth Magazine named Mike to "The Top 100 Wealth Advisors" list. Mike is a charter member of Ed Slott's Master Elite IRA Advisor Group and served as a consultant on Ed's most recent book "Stay Rich for Life" as seen on PBS. Mike holds the Series 24, 7, 66 and Life and Health Insurance licenses. Mike is a registered representative of American Portfolios Services, Inc.—member FINRA & SIPC and an Investment Advisor Representative of American Portfolios Advisors, Inc., a SEC Registered Investment Advisor. This is his second book.

JOHN DALEY, AIF

John began his career in the financial services industry in 1998 as a currency option broker with Cantor-Fitzgerald in the World Trade Center. John has earned the Accredited Investment Fiduciary (AIF) designation through the Center for Fiduciary Studies at the Katz School of Business. John has a Bachelor's Degree in Business Economics, and he earned a Master's in Accounting from SUNY Albany. He has served as an Adjunct Professor in the Lally School of Management and Technology at RPI and the MBA and Master's of Tax Program at SUNY Albany. John also taught professional courses for the Chartered Financial Analyst and Certified Public Accountant designations. John holds the Series 7, 66 and Life and Health Insurance licenses. John is a registered representative of American Portfolios Services, Inc.—member FINRA & SIPC and an Investment Advisor Representative of American Portfolios Advisors, Inc., a SEC Registered Investment Advisor. This is his first book.

INDEX

For information on booking authors Dean Barber, Michael E. Brown or John Daley as keynote speakers for your next conference, meeting, or company event, or to order additional copies of *Retire a Winner!* for your employees and/or clients, please contact their respective offices:

- ❏ Dean Barber
  Barber Financial Group
  Office: 913.393.1000 • Toll Free: 888.848.8003
  retire@barberfinancialgroup.com

- ❏ Michael E. Brown
  Madison Wealth Managers
  Office: 518.348.7770 • Toll Free: 888.376.6460
  info@madisonmanagers.com

- ❏ John Daley
  Madison Wealth Managers
  Office: 518.348.7770 • Toll Free: 888.376.6460
  info@madisonmanagers.com